Perspectives on Drug Use in the United States

Perspectives on Drug Use in the United States

Bernard Segal, Ph.D.
Editor

The Haworth Press
New York • London

Perspectives on Drug Use in the United States has also been published as *Drugs & Society*, Volume 1, Number 1, Fall 1986.

The Haworth Press, Inc., 28 East 22 Street, New York, NY 10010-6194
EUROSPAN/Haworth, 3 Henrietta Street, London WC2E 8LU England

Library of Congress Cataloging in Publication Data

Perspectives on drug use in the United States.

Published also as Drugs & Society, v. 1, no., 1, fall 1986.
Includes bibliographies.
1. Drug abuse—United States. 2. Narcotics, Control of—United States. I. Segal, Bernard. [DNLM: 1. Drugs. 2. Legislation, Drug—United States. 3. Substance Abuse. WM 270 P4673]
HV5825.P37 1986 362.2′9′0973 86-7615
ISBN 0-86656-586-8

Perspectives on Drug Use in the United States

Drugs & Society
Volume 1, Number 1

CONTENTS

Preface

Given the plethora of journals in substance abuse, why a new one? Part of the answer is that most of the contemporary literature is chiefly concerned with publishing research reports. Many of the studies that are reported, with few exceptions, are not tied to a theory or model, and fewer present findings which have direct application to practitioners. A large number of studies have also consisted of unrelated studies yielding, in many instances, inconsistent, contradictory or piecemeal findings. Fewer are critically reviewed. Oftentimes these research reports are so burdened with documentation to support findings or to justify statements that the reader is distracted from appreciating the contents of the article.

Drugs & Society is intended to provide a contrast to the traditional journal format and content and will provide stimulating, provocative reports that will critically review issues and provide direction for research; it will also report research findings in a creative manner, and the research cited will have direct implications for practitioners and researchers. First and foremost, however, *Drugs & Society* will concentrate on reviewing contemporary issues in the field of substance abuse. In so doing, *Drugs & Society* will break away from traditional journal formats and procedures in order to give authors the greatest possible latitude to express their ideas. The journal's aim is to serve as a forum for the presentation of reports and discussion of issues that currently prevail in the field of substance abuse.

Beginning with this first issue, *Drugs & Society* presents a series of articles that address several important issues. The first report, "Drug Laws and Drug Law Enforcement," by Edward Brecher, examines how effective drug laws and enforcement policies have been in combating drug abuse in the United States. Brecher's rather scathing conclusions on the effect of drug control policies and procedures should help to stimulate interest in a more detailed examination of the effect of drug control policies, and in exploring what direction future legislation and enforcement policies might follow to be more effective.

The second article, "The Deviance Model of Drug-Taking

Behavior: A Critique,'' by Charles Winick, presents a critical review of the effectiveness of the deviance model, and provides suggestions to help revise the model to better account for different forms of drug use among different types of users. Franklin Shontz and James Spotts, in the third paper, titled, ''Who Are the Drug Users?'', present a narrative-like review of their research that focuses on identifying the psychological characteristics of drug users. They make a compelling case for the utilization of the individual case study method as a valid procedure that will provide useful and relevant information about drug users that will further an understanding of ''who are the drug users.''

''Women: Alcohol and Other Drugs,'' by Edith S. Lisansky Gomberg, the next article, presents a comprehensive review of the historical and contemporary issues concerning women and drugs. She notes that the study of women and drug use has only just begun, and, following her review of the issues, provides a discussion of specific women-related research questions that are in need of further research.

The final paper, ''Perspectives on Drug Use in the United States,'' by Louise Richards, examines drug use in a cultural-anthropological context, one that departs from traditional psychosocial discussions of drug abuse. By reviewing drug use and abuse in this context, Dr. Richards provides a perspective that accounts for the use and abuse of legal, illicit and prescriptive drugs as part of a ''new'' drug-oriented culture that has emerged in the United States. Her review has important implications for prevention of drug abuse.

In all, this first issue of *Drugs & Society* is a compilation of articles that deal with important issues and concerns that have a direct bearing on the formation of drug control policies and procedures and on the direction of future research.

I would like to acknowledge and express my appreciation for the thoughtful assistance provided by Janine Dorsey, who deserves the title of Editorial Assistant because of her careful and critical review of each manuscript. Linda Norman's assistance in typing and helping to finalize the manuscripts is also greatly appreciated.

Bernard Segal

Perspectives on Drug Use in the United States

Drug Laws and Drug Law Enforcement: A Review and Evaluation Based on 111 Years of Experience

Edward M. Brecher

ABSTRACT. The problem of drug use and abuse has been present in American society ever since its inception, and many different laws have been enacted, both at the federal and state level, to combat drug use. The question that arises is how effective have these laws been or what has their impact been on reducing drug use within the United States? This paper undertakes a critical review and evaluation of the effects of drug legislation and enforcement policies and practices over the past 111 years. It is concluded that drug use has not been reduced by the enactment of anti-drug laws and the actions of law enforcement agencies. The reasons for this failure and why continued failure will occur are discussed.

INTRODUCTION

Back in the 19th century, all drugs in the United States were licit drugs and could be legally sold over the counter without a prescription.[1] Opium, morphine, heroin, cocaine, and marijuana were among the licit drugs. Indeed, the opiates "were as freely accessible as aspirin is today."[2] But there was one exception: smoking opium in San Francisco "smoking-houses" or "opium dens" was banned by an 1875 city ordinance.[3]

Since 1875, literally hundreds of additional city ordinances, state laws, and federal laws and regulations have been enacted for the curbing of drug use in the United States. Vast resources of money and manpower have been expended, decade after decade, in efforts to enforce these laws. But only rarely does anyone pause to ask, *what have our anti-drug laws and law enforcement efforts accomplished during the 111 years since 1875?*

Edward M. Brecher, Yelping Hill, West Cornwall, CT.

This review addresses this question, drawing chiefly from three major sources which are described below.

1. In 1928, Dr. Charles E. Terry of the Rockefeller-funded Committee on Drug Addictions, Bureau of Social Hygiene, and his associate, Mildred Pellens, published a monumental 1,042 page report entitled *The Opium Problem*, which cogently reviewed and summarized the United States experience up to that time;[4]
2. My own 1972 study entitled, *Licit and Illicit Drugs: A Consumers Union Report on Narcotics, Stimulants, Depressants, Inhalants, Hallucinogens, and Marijuana—Including Caffeine, Nicotine, and Alcohol*;[5] and
3. Information disseminated by the United States Drug Enforcement Administration (DEA),[6] and by the National Narcotics Intelligence Consumers Committee (NNICC),[7] a joint organization of the DEA and ten other federal agencies concerned with drug problems and drug law enforcement.

This review will describe how the nation's drug problem thus far has not been solved by anti-drug laws and through the efforts of law enforcement agencies. In fact, I shall discuss how these efforts have exacerbated drug problems and describe some of the reasons why law enforcement efforts have invariably failed to curb illicit drug availability throughout the past 111 years of drug use in our country. I will also point out why such efforts will inevitably continue to fail.

OPIUM SMOKING

The tens of thousands of Chinese men and boys "imported" into the United States during the 1850s and 1860s to build the Western railroads brought opium smoking with them. Opium smoking, as the Chinese had learned centuries earlier, was, for two main reasons, the blandest and least hazardous mode of securing a morphine effect. First, the type of opium used, known as "smoking opium," was of a specially weak type containing only nine percent morphine or less, and second, only about one-tenth of the morphine in this weak opium enters the vapor, and only a portion of the morphine vapor enters the human blood stream when inhaled. Thus, the so-called opium smoker is in fact a vapor inhaler; there are no tars or other carcinogens involved. Even a heavy inhaler of smoking opium—one who smokes 25 pills a day—gets barely the equivalent of a single dose of injected morphine or heroin. The modest dose from smoking, moreover, reaches the bloodstream over a considerable span of time rather than instantaneously, as when morphine or heroin is mainlined.[8]

The San Francisco city fathers had nothing against opium smoking in 1875 and did not try to ban it; they only sought to curb opium smoking in Chinese opium dens. "Many [white] women and young girls, as well as young men of good family, were being induced to visit the dens, where they were ruined morally and otherwise." The 1875 ordinance was designed to terminate this inter-racial fraternization.[9]

The ordinance provided heavy penalties: fines or imprisonment, or both. "Many arrests were made and the punishment was prompt and thorough." As a result, "the vice was indulged in much less openly, but nonetheless extensively; for although the larger smoking houses were closed, the small dens in Chinatown were well patronized, and the vice grew surely and steadily." Indeed, the new law "seemed to add zest to their enjoyment."[10]

Despite this unexpected effect of helping to further popularize opium smoking that occurred after enactment of the pioneering San Francisco ordinance restricting opium use, 27 other cities and several states followed San Francisco's example during the next few decades. Opium, however, was still able to be legally imported, and the following statistics, which show the level of opium importation between 1860 and 1909, provide an important yardstick which can be used to evaluate how effective the first anti-drug laws were.[11]

Years	Pounds of smoking opium imported
1860–1869	21,176
1870–1879	48,049
1880–1889	85,988
1890–1899	92,462
1900–1909	148,168

As can be noted from the years cited above, the importation of opium increased steadily despite the proliferation of state and local laws banning its use.

In 1909, Congress stepped in to outlaw the importation of smoking opium.[12] Although this resulted in a "cut off" of legally imported opium, it did not cut off the opium supply. Instead, it opened the door of opportunity for a new and highly profitable career: the career of the drug smuggler. As late as 1930, according to Federal Narcotics Commissioner Harry J. Anslinger, "opium dens could be found in almost every American city."[13]

But opium is a bulky drug. As law enforcement techniques became more sophisticated, the smugglers shifted from opium to morphine and then to heroin, a more potent opiate that yields more doses per pound and per cubic inch, and therefore, higher profits per shipment. Opium smokers were compelled to follow the lead of the smugglers:

> Case 35, now thirty-eight years of age, started smoking opium twenty years ago [in 1905]. After the importation of opium was prevented by law, he used morphine; and when this could no longer be secured, he shifted to heroin.[14]

Thus, the net effect of city, state, and federal efforts to stamp out opium smoking over a period of more than half a century was to convert opium smokers to heroin main-liners. This change was not for the better.

The anti-opium-smoking laws, like all subsequent anti-drug laws, had one central weakness: they were aimed at private transactions between willing sellers and willing, usually eager, buyers. Hence, there were no complainants. The philosopher Baruch Spinoza (1632–1677) explained why such laws inevitably fail:

> All laws which can be violated without doing any one an injury are laughed at. Nay, so far are they from doing anything to control the desires and passions of men that, on the contrary, they direct and incite men's thoughts the more toward those very objects; for we always strive toward what is forbidden and desire the things we are not allowed to have. And men of leisure are never deficient in the ingenuity needed to enable them to outwit laws framed to regulate things which cannot be entirely forbidden. . . . He who tries to determine everything by law will foment crime rather than lessen it.[15]

THE HARRISON NARCOTIC ACT (1914)

During the 19th century, Americans took in their stride the fact that many of their fellow citizens used opium or morphine, but they worried about the opium problem in China. After 1900, they similarly worried about opium in our new possession, the Philippines. Hence, President Theodore Roosevelt called an international opium conference in 1906 and another in 1911, out of which came the Hague Convention of 1912, an international treaty obligating each signatory country to regulate the opium traffic within its borders. Congress was urged to pass the Harrison Narcotic Act of 1914 to fulfill our treaty obligations.[16]

On its face, the 1914 law merely provided for the orderly marketing of opium, morphine, heroin, and cocaine (which was mistakenly classified as a narcotic). Manufacturers, importers, pharmacists, and physicians were to be licensed to deal in or prescribe narcotics on payment of a moderate fee. Patent medicine manufacturers were exempted even from the licensing and fee provisions, provided they limited themselves to ''preparations and remedies which do not contain more than two grains of opium, or more than one-fourth of a grain of morphine, or more than one-eighth of a grain of heroin . . . in one avoirdupois ounce.''[17]

The law further specified:

> Nothing contained in this section shall apply . . . to the dispensing or distribution of any of the aforesaid drugs to a patient by a physician, dentist, or veterinary surgeon registered under this Act in the course of his professional practice only.[18]

Following the passage of the Act, however, federal prosecutors decreed that what purported to be a licensing law was in fact a prohibition law. Physicians, for example, were arrested and brought to trial for prescribing opiates to addicts—on the ground that such prescriptions were not written ''in the course of professional practice.''[19]

The new law became effective in April, 1915, and within six weeks its first effects were clearly visible. The *New York Medical Journal* reported on May 15:

> As was expected . . . the immediate effects of the Harrison

> anti-narcotic law were seen in the flocking of drug habitués to hospitals and sanitoriums. Sporadic crimes of violence were reported, too, due usually to desperate efforts by addicts to obtain drugs, but occasionally to a delirious state induced by sudden withdrawal. . . .
>
> The really serious results of this legislation, however, will only appear gradually and will not always be recognized as such. These will be the failures of promising careers, the disrupting of happy families, the commission of crimes which will never be traced to their real cause, and the influx into hospitals for the mentally disordered of many who would otherwise live socially competent lives.[20]

Six months later, an editorial in *American Medicine* added:

> Instead of improving conditions, the laws recently passed have made the problem more complex. Honest medical men have found such handicaps and dangers to themselves and their reputations in these laws . . . that they have simply decided to have as little to do as possible with drug addicts or their needs. . . . The druggists are in the same position and for similar reasons many of them have discontinued entirely the sale of narcotic drugs. [The addict] is denied the medical care he urgently needs, open, above-board sources from which he formerly obtained his drug supply are closed to him, and he is driven to the underworld where he can get his drug, but of course, surreptitiously and in violation of the law . . .
>
> Abuses in the sale of narcotic drugs are increasing. . . .[21]

In 1922, while British authorities were pondering whether to follow the American example and outlaw narcotics, one of their number, Dr. Harry Campbell, came to see for himself how the Harrison Act was working. He was amazed and disgusted by what he saw:

> In the United States of America a drug addict is regarded as a malefactor even though the habit has been acquired through the medicinal use of the drug, as in the case, e.g., of American soldiers who were gassed and otherwise maimed in the Great War [World War I]. The Harrison Narcotic Law . . . places

> severe restrictions upon the sale of narcotics and upon the medical profession, and necessitated the appointment of a whole army of officials. In consequence of this stringent law a vast clandestine commerce in narcotics has grown up in that country. The small bulk of these drugs renders the evasion of the law comparatively easy, and the country is overrun by an army of peddlers who extort exhorbitant prices from their helpless victims. It appears that not only has the Harrison Law failed to diminish the number of drug takers—some contend, indeed, that it has increased their number—but, far from bettering the lot of the opiate addict, it has actually worsened it; for without curtailing the supply of the drug it has sent the price up tenfold, and this has had the effect of impoverishing the poorer class of addicts and reducing them to a condition of such abject misery as to render them incapable of gaining an honest livelihood.[22]

These were not just isolated comments. Almost all observers from 1915 to 1985 have continuously agreed that U.S. anti-drug laws are not working. But instead of drawing the obvious conclusions—that anti-drug laws can't work, and that we need a better approach to our drug problems—most observers have called instead for even stricter laws and even more zealous law enforcement.

"TIGHTENING UP" THE HARRISON ACT

In 1922, when the failure of the Harrison Act was already clearly visible, Congress concluded that the maximum penalty for violating the law—five years in prison—was too mild; so the maximum service was escalated to ten years in prison. Subsequent state laws modeled on the Harrison Act decreed 20-year, 40-year, and even 99-year maximum sentences. Life imprisonment and the death sentence were added to both state and federal anti-narcotics laws during the 1950s.[23] These increased penalties, however, did not close down the illicit drug market. Instead, they acted as an opiate on public opinion, persuading the innocent public that severe measures were at last being taken against drug traffickers.

When long maximum sentences failed to eliminate drug use, the blame was placed on "soft-hearted" judges who refused to invoke the extreme penalties. So, high *minimum* sentences were decreed, including life imprisonment as a minimum sentence. Under these provisions judges were *required* to sentence offenders for life if they were convicted of specified offenses, such as providing opiates to minors. Some federal and state anti-drug laws also specified that drug offenders should be ineligible for probation, suspension of sentence, or parole.[24]

The first federal offender sentenced under the life imprisonment without parole provision was a 21-year-old, born in Mexico, epileptic, with an I.Q. of 59, who had been recently released from a state mental hospital. He was charged with procuring a small amount of heroin for another addict, a 17-year-old employed as an *agent provocateur* by the U.S. Department of Justice. It was the feeble-minded offender's first federal offense and his first narcotics offense.[25] His imprisonment for life can hardly have contributed much to solving the country's drug problem.

When heavier sentences failed to curb the underground market in opiates and other illicit drugs, state and federal laws were amended to make convictions easier. It was no longer necessary to show that money had changed hands, for example, in order to secure a conviction for "sale" of drugs. Possessing narcotics "with intent to sell" became a crime punishable by imprisonment, even though no drugs were in fact sold. New York State even made it a crime to "loiter for the purpose of using narcotics," even though no narcotics were used, and possession of a hypodermic syringe or needle became a crime even in the absence of drugs.[26] The ostensible purpose of all these laws and law enforcement efforts was to cut down the number of drug addicts.

It is possible to gauge how much has been accomplished in limiting opiate use by comparing the number of addicts prior to passage of the Harrison Act with the number today. By far the best estimate of addicts back in 1914 was prepared for the U.S. Public Health Service by Drs. Lawrence Kolb and A. G. DuMez in 1924. They used data from city-wide and state-wide surveys, from duties paid on opiate imports, from the examination of army recruits, and from other sources. They showed that the number of opium, morphine, and heroin addicts in 1914 was certainly less than 246,000, and probably in the vicinity of 215,000.[27]

The U.S. Drug Enforcement Administration (DEA) makes similar estimates nowadays. The latest available DEA estimate for 1983 is 492,000 *heroin* addicts.[28] Thus, the net outcome of drug law enforcement, 70 years after the Harrison Narcotic Act, has been to shift opium addicts and morphine addicts to heroin, and to double the number of addicts.

THE ECONOMICS OF THE BLACK MARKET

The "American system of narcotics distribution" was developed during the 1920s and progressively improved by the "distributors" thereafter. While there have no doubt been many changes in detail, this remarkably ingenious system still survives today. Here, in rough outline, is how the system works, using heroin as an example.[29] (The cocaine and marijuana marketing systems are similar in principle.)

Pure heroin is smuggled into the United States from many countries, at a price that varies from year to year and even from month to month. For the purposes of this model, let us say that the importer buys it, landed in the U.S., for $10,000 a kilogram (2.2 pounds). A moderate dose of heroin is ten milligrams; hence, there are 100,000 doses in a kilogram. At $10 a dose, the kilogram of heroin that costs the importer $10,000 yields $1,000,000 at the street level—more in some cities in some years, less at other times and elsewhere.[30] In any year, everywhere in the United States, there is no lack of the profit motive for dealing in heroin, cocaine, and marijuana. The "profit motive," after all, is the "American way."

Since drug trafficking is a risky business, traffickers limit their sales to only a few customers whom they know and trust. An importer may sell to only eight wholesalers, each wholesaler to only six retailers, each retailer to only six pushers, and each pusher to only 15 users—yet the supplies from one importer will reach 4,320 users.[31] If each user spends only $20 a day for heroin, the profits at every level are substantial:

—The street pusher collects $300 a day, or $110,000 a year, from 15 users. He pays the dealer $35,000, reaping a $75,000 a year profit.

—Each dealer collects $210,000 a year from his six pushers, and pays $100,000 a year to his wholesaler, reaping a profit of $110,000 per year.

—Each wholesaler collects $600,000 a year from his six dealers, and pays his importer $300,000, reaping a profit of $300,000 a year.
—Each importer collects $1,800,000 a year from his six wholesalers for heroin that cost him $1,000,000, reaping a profit of $800,000 a year.[32]

Since taxes are rarely paid on illicit drug profits the incentives are substantially greater than these figures would suggest. And except at the street level, the work is ridiculously easy. Consider, for example, the life of the dealer who nets $110,000 a year for passing heroin from a wholesaler to six pushers.

During the early years of the Harrison Narcotic Act, the narcotics police concentrated their attention on street pushers. These were relatively easy to catch; but for every pusher arrested, there were 15 users eager to take his place.

Efforts have accordingly been made to penetrate higher into the chain of distribution. Sometimes these efforts succeed and we read in the newspapers of gargantuan "drug busts." The effect is only temporary, however, for there are always wholesalers waiting to become importers, and dealers waiting to become wholesalers, and pushers waiting to become dealers. No college degree is required, and even members of ethnic minorities can sometimes find a place in the trafficking hierarchy.

What the drug busts do accomplish is to maintain high prices, or even to raise prices higher. At first the narcotics police pointed to higher prices as evidence of their success, but they eventually learned better. When prices go up addicts must steal more. A rise in price also produces a rise in profits, and thus increases the incentives attracting newcomers to drug-trafficking careers. Despite 70 years of intensive efforts to curb drug trafficking by arresting importers, wholesalers, dealers, and pushers, the American system of drug distribution has not only survived, but has expanded.

CLOSING THE BORDERS TO SMUGGLING

Disillusioned with the failure of efforts to curb domestic trafficking, the federal narcotics police through the decades have placed increasing emphasis on closing the U.S. borders to drug smuggling.

In *Licit and Illicit Drugs*, I explained why the U.S. borders cannot be closed.[33] I used heroin as an example, but the same principles apply to cocaine and marijuana today, as they did in 1971:

—In 1971, smugglers were supplying an estimated 250,000 addicts with daily doses of heroin. This required the smuggling of about four tons of heroin per year. Total U.S. imports of all products at that time exceeded 100,000,000 tons a year. The task of the Bureau of Customs, accordingly, was to find four tons of heroin amid 100,000,000 tons of other imports.[34]

—Four million travelers in those days entered the U.S. each week. Half a dozen of them could smuggle in a week's supply of heroin (170 pounds) for the entire country. The task of border guards, accordingly, was to spot half a dozen heroin smugglers each week among the 4,000,000 other border crossers.[35]

Though the figures have no doubt changed a bit the border problem remains essentially the same today.

The economic effect of even an enormous seizure of smuggled drugs, moreover, is only minimal, as a hypothetical example will show:

—Suppose that one kilo of pure heroin, awaiting export to the U.S., is valued at $5,000. Safely landed in the U.S., the value rises to $10,000. The street value is $1,000,000.

—In an average or typical year, the narcotics police and customs agents seize an estimated five percent of all heroin destined for the U.S. This means that 1.0525 kilos of heroin worth $5,263 must be exported to the U.S. in order to land safely one kilo with a street value of $1,000,000.

—If, as a result of Herculean efforts and unprecedented good luck, the narcotics police and customs agents should in some future year seize 50 percent of all heroin destined for the U.S., it would be necessary for foreign suppliers to export 2 kilos of heroin, valued at $10,000, in order to land safely one kilo with a street value of $1,000,000.

In an ordinary year, customs officials intercept perhaps five percent of the heroin destined for U.S. traffickers, or 200 kilos during the year. This means that 4,200 kilos must be shipped in order for 4,000 kilos to be safely landed. The heroin seized adds about a penny to the average cost of a dose of heroin on the city streets. If, by a Herculean effort, the narcotics police manage to double their seizures, an additional penny per dose is added to the cost of street heroin.[36]

Finally, policing our borders to intercept smuggled drugs has a selective effect in maintaining prices high enough to keep the system operating, for consider the fate of an importer who dares to cut prices. His competitors will no doubt frown on such tactics. The Bureau of Customs will receive an anonymous tip. Law enforcement authorities will proudly announce a huge seizure, and the price cutting will come to an abrupt halt.[37]

COCAINE AND THE AMPHETAMINES

When 16th century Spanish conquistadores invaded the Inca Empire (now Peru, Bolivia, Ecuador, and parts of Chile and Columbia) they found that the natives chewed the leaves of the coca plant much as Americans now drink coffee, and for the same reason. The cocaine in coca leaves is, like caffeine, a stimulant of the central nervous system. Drinks made from the coca leaves, including Coca Cola, became popular throughout the world.

The Harrison Narcotic Act mistakenly labeled cocaine as a narcotic; hence, the same Draconian penalties decreed for heroin trafficking applied also to cocaine. Smugglers and peddlers nevertheless maintained a flourishing black market in cocaine for many years.

Beginning about 1932, however, a group of synthetic stimulants, the amphetamines, became available.[38] They had notable advantages over cocaine. One advantage was price. As late as the 1950s legally manufactured amphetamine tablets could be purchased at wholesale for $7.50 per 1,000—three-quarters of a cent per dose.[39] Cocaine could not compete. Faced with cut-rate amphetamine competition, the market for imported cocaine withered away after 1940. By 1965, amphetamines were ubiquitously available from four sources:

a. Physicians prescribed them to patients;
b. Legally manufactured amphetamines were diverted to the illicit market;
c. Legal supplies were also exported to Mexico and then smuggled back to the U.S. for illicit distribution;

d. Clandestine "speed labs" in the U.S. were manufacturing illicit amphetamines for as little as half a cent per dose, undercutting the legitimate manufacturers.[40]

Congress responded in 1965 by "tightening up" the anti-amphetamine laws, and thereafter all four of the amphetamine sources were under increasing law enforcement pressure. Physicians who wrote suspicious numbers of amphetamine prescriptions were being visited by state and federal narcotics agents and some were being prosecuted. The U.S. Bureau of Customs enhanced its surveillance of smuggled amphetamines. The Bureau of Narcotics & Dangerous Drugs (now the DEA), as well as the FDA and state and local police agencies, joined forces against both the diversion of legal amphetamines and the illicit speed labs. Efforts were made to curb the supply of raw materials needed for amphetamine manufacture by the speed labs. By 1969 the street price of amphetamines had been driven so high that, for the first time in thirty years, it became profitable once more to deal in cocaine.[41]

"More and more cocaine, worth millions of dollars," the *New York Times* reported in 1970, "is being smuggled into the United States from Latin America."[42] A federal narcotics agent was quoted as saying: "The traffic in cocaine is growing by leaps and bounds. It was insignificant only a few years ago, but now it has become a significant problem." A New York State narcotics agent was quoted as explaining why cocaine was becoming so popular: "because younger users are finding out about it. The kids are beginning to learn it's pretty much like speed."[43]

The Federal Bureau of Narcotics estimated that in 1969 an enormous amount of cocaine, 900 kilograms, was smuggled into the United States—enough for 18,000,000 doses. Since then, of course, the war against cocaine has been unremitting. New and ingenious techniques for curbing smuggling and distribution within the country have been developed; both federal and state anti-narcotics forces have been beefed up and law enforcement appropriations have increased. According to official DEA estimates, however, the amount of cocaine smuggled into the U.S. zoomed from 900 kilograms in 1969 to at least 75,000 kilograms, and perhaps as much as 95,000 kilograms by 1984.[45] The rapidly expanding U.S. cocaine market, indeed, was oversupplied by 1984, and prices were beginning to drop a bit.

THE MARIJUANA TAX ACT (1937)

The Jamestown settlers brought the marijuana plant, commonly known as hemp, to North America in 1611, and throughout the colonial period, hemp fiber was an important export. Indeed, in 1762, "Virginia awarded bounties for hemp culture and manufacture, and imposed penalties on those who did not produce it." George Washington grew hemp at Mount Vernon. Its medicinal uses were known: *Extractum Cannabis*, or Extract of Hemp U.S.P., was an accepted drug in the *U.S. Pharmacopeia* until 1942.[46]

There were only sporadic accounts of marijuana smoking for recreational purposes, however, until 1920, when Alcohol Prohibition was enacted. Then, modest marijuana markets sprang up in New Orleans, New York, and a few other cities.[47] In 1933, Federal Narcotics Commissioner Harry J. Anglinger launched a one-man war against marijuana. By 1937, at his behest, 46 of the 48 states had anti-marijuana laws, and in that year he also urged Congress to pass the Marijuana Tax Act modeled on the Harrison Act.[48]

The American Medical Association (AMA) led the vigorous opposition to the Anslinger proposal. An editorial in the *Journal of the American Medical Association*, explained why:

> After more than twenty years of federal effort and the expenditure of millions of dollars, the opium and cocaine habits are still widespread. The best efforts of an efficient bureau of narcotics, supplemented by the efforts of an equally efficient bureau of customs, have failed to stop the unlawful flow of opium and coca leaves and their compounds and derivatives, on which the continuance and spread of narcotic addiction depends. . . . What reason is there, then, for believing that any better results can be obtained by direct federal efforts to suppress a habit arising out of the misuse of such a drug as cannabis? Certainly it is almost as easy to smuggle into the country and to distribute as are opium and coca leaves. Moreover it can be cultivated in many parts of the United States and grows wild in field and forest and along the highways in many places.[49]

Despite these and many other qualms, the Marijuana Tax Act was passed in 1937. As the AMA had predicted, the Act failed to curb marijuana use. Accordingly, both Congress and the state legislatures (as they had with opiates) escalated the penalties for possession and sale of marijuana. Here are some of the penalties in effect on January 1, 1970:

—A first federal conviction for selling marijuana brought a mandatory minimum sentence of five years for a first offense and 10 for a second; terms of 20 years for a first offense and 40 for a second were possible. Probation, parole, and suspended sentences were denied to *all* marijuana offenders—even those convicted for the first time of *possessing* a single marijuana joint.

—In Georgia, sale of marijuana to a minor was punishable by life imprisonment, even if it was a first offense—though the jury could recommend ten-to-twenty years instead. A second such offense was punishable by death—but the jury could recommend life imprisonment or ten-to-twenty years instead. No mitigation of sentences (suspension, probation, or parole) was permitted.

—In Illinois, the penalty for a first-sale offense was not less than ten years and as much as life. A mandatory life sentence was in effect for a second-sale offense.

—In Louisiana, an adult selling marijuana to another adult was subject to a minimum mandatory sentence of ten years at hard labor and a maximum sentence of fifty years at hard labor for a first offense. If the buyer were under twenty-one, a first-sale offense required a mandatory minimum sentence of thirty years at hard labor and could draw a death sentence. No suspended sentence or probation was permitted.

—In Massachusetts, it was a felony punishable by not more than five years in prison to be in a place where marijuana was kept or deposited, or to be in the company of anyone known to be in illegal possession of marijuana.

—In Missouri, the judge could hand down a life sentence for a second-possession offense or a first-sale offense, without possibility of suspended sentence, probation, or parole. If the buyer were a minor, a death sentence was possible for a first-sale offense.

—In Texas, the judge could impose a life sentence for a first-possession offense.

—In Utah, a life sentence was possible for a first marijuana sale offense or for a second possession-with-intent-to-sell offense.[50]

Draconian penalties, however, had unanticipated consequences. Juries were likely to acquit if they learned that conviction for a minor offense meant long, perhaps lifelong, imprisonment without parole. Instead of plea-bargaining, offenders demanded a jury trial, thus overburdening the prosecutors and jamming up the courts. After 1970, as more and more children of legislators and children of the friends of legislators were charged under these laws, the penalties were de-escalated, especially for *possession* offenses. But efforts to curtail the importation, cultivation, and distribution of marijuana continued unabated.

No estimates are available for consumption of marijuana prior to the Marijuana Tax Act of 1937 and the satellite state laws—a few tons a year or less would be as good a guess as any. The DEA has reasonably good estimates for the 1980s, however, at least 9,600 tons in 1981, rising to at least 12,340 tons in 1982, at least 13,600 tons in 1983, and at least 15,000 tons in 1984, which included both domestic and imported supplies.[51]

OPERATION INTERCEPT

Every year or two, some Congressman with a short memory proposes that the United States try something new in its war against drugs: mobilize the U.S. Army, the U.S. Navy, the U.S. Air Force, and the U.S. Coast Guard to seal our borders. Those with longer memories are less enthusiastic.

Richard Nixon became President in January, 1969, and during that summer he authorized military participation in closing the Mexican border.[52] "At the direction of President Nixon," Felix Belair, Jr., reported from Washington on September 9, 1969, "federal enforcement agencies are preparing an all-out drive on the smuggling of drugs into the United States from Mexico. Details of the drive are being kept a closely guarded secret . . . "

Belair then went on to give some of the closely guarded details. "On this side of the border, pursuit planes and some motor torpedo boats will be employed for the first time. Additional observation planes will be placed at the disposal of a strengthened border patrol," in what Belair correctly described as "the nation's largest peacetime search and seizure operation."[53]

Two weeks later, Belair revealed where the planes and boats

were coming from: "Military pursuit planes borrowed from the Air Force are poised to chase any aircraft. . . . The surveillance network was spread out to sea, with Navy boats plying the Gulf of Mexico and a variety of patrol craft in coastal waters." Borrowed radars, mounted on trucks, were posted to spot approaching planes that had failed to file flight plans. On the ground, more than 2,000 agents were mobilized, including many borrowed from other ports of entry. This, of course, weakened law enforcement at other ports.[54]

Operation Intercept was brilliantly timed. A drought in Mexico had already curtailed the supply of U.S. marijuana, most of which came from Mexico in those days. The operation began at 2:30 p.m., on Sunday afternoon, when American tourists attending Mexican horse races and bullfights would be returning. By late afternoon, traffic was backed up for six miles in the border dust and heat. "Halted motorists expressed their feeling in the classical manner" by blowing their horns. "They're playing our song," one customs agent was quoted as saying.

Ordinarily, border agents were expected to clear vehicles at the rate of one per minute. During Operation Intercept, the quota was lowered to one every two or three minutes. This change was sufficient to disrupt border traffic, but hardly enough for thorough searches.

Requiring border crossers to strip to the skin and submit to a body search was a much-publicized feature of the operation. During the first week there were 1,824 body searches, leaving roughly 1,978,000 persons who crossed the border without being stripped and searched.[55]

The success of Operation Intercept was announced on the seventh day by a federal spokesman, despite the fact that arrests had averaged less than five per day and little contraband had been seized. "We're measuring our success not by the quantity of seizures made, but by the price of marijuana, heroin, and other drugs on the market," a federal spokesman explained. "No large seizures have been made because obviously the big smugglers have gotten the word." Obviously, the small smugglers had also gotten the word.

One effect of Operation Intercept, that still persists in 1985, was to alert smugglers to the Achilles' heel of radar. "Recently positioned radar installations . . . show the blips of intruding aircraft from the south," the *New York Times* explained, "but the blips faded from the scanning screen as the planes dropped between mountain ranges and canyon corridors or passed beyond range . . . " Armed with this knowledge, smugglers actually increased their use of cross-border planes. "They fly low and slow, by the light of the moon, and make $50,000 a night," the *New York Times* reported more than a year after Operation Intercept was discontinued. A customs agent was quoted as conceding: "Anyone who knows how to fly can get into the business and make a lot of money. . . . They're developing their own air force, and it's getting bigger and bigger." At first small planes were used, but following Operation Intercept, "a lot of them are starting to use bigger planes—DC-3s, surplus military transports . . . and we have our eye on one group that has a Constellation."[56] A Constellation can carry 20 tons of cargo—enough to supply the entire U.S. heroin market for four or five years with cargo from a single flight.

A second durable effect of Operation Intercept was to introduce young people to other drugs during the brief period when marijuana was hard to get. A survey of 478 undergraduates and graduate students at the University of California at Los Angeles, for example, noted that "76 percent of the students . . . reported that they increased their consumption of one or more other drugs (including alcohol) because of the unavailability of marijuana."[57]

A third very-durable effect was that the cultivation of marijuana in the U.S. was stimulated.[58]

The most acute and dramatic effect, however, was to trigger a flood of outraged protests from Mexico, from other Latin American countries, from tradespeople in Texas, New Mexico, Arizona, and California, whose business was being ruined by the border jam-ups, and from congressmen and senators representing those constituents.[59] President Diaz of Mexico labeled the operation a "bureaucratic error" that had "raised a wall of suspicion between Mexico and the United States."[60] The head of an association of border cities mobilized local protest and also sent telegrams to chambers of commerce throughout the United States, urging them to protest, and warning them that "time is short and the need for action is immediate." In an interview, he added: "The economic life's blood of these communities is based on a free flow of vehicular and pedestrian traffic in both directions. Interrupt that flow and the economy dies, people are thrown out of work, and the communities will become ghost towns."[61]

After twenty days of such protests, the Nixon Administration caved in. Traffic across the border began flowing freely again on October 11, 1969.[62]

CURBING DRUG PRODUCTION ABROAD

After the 1969 failure of Operation Intercept, our narcotics police continued to go through the motions, but U.S. policy-setting officials no longer had confidence that law enforcement could either seal our borders or disrupt our domestic system of illicit drug distribution. Instead, they enthusiastically turned in 1970 to a new strategy, one which remains today at the forefront of the U.S. war on drugs: efforts to persuade, dragoon, or bribe foreign countries to curb their production of illicit drugs destined for the U.S. market.

Turkey, for several reasons, was an almost ideal first target for this new strategy. Turkish opium poppies supplied the raw material for almost all illicit U.S. heroin during the 1960s. Turkey was receiving more than $100,000,000 a year in U.S. military and civilian aid. This aid could be curtailed if Turkey failed to curb poppy-growing, or increased if the government cooperated. As a military dictatorship, Turkey could institute strong measures without the niceties of due process or civil liberties.[63]

This new anti-drug strategy proved amazingly successful. Turkish poppies today contribute at most a negligible trickle of opium for the U.S. heroin trade. The result, however, has *not* been to curb the availability of heroin. Rather, the Turkish retreat opened the door of opportunity to poppy growers in Afghanistan, Burma, India, Laos, Lebanon, Mexico, Pakistan, and Thailand—the eight countries which, according to the DEA, now share among themselves the U.S. heroin market formerly monopolized by Turkey.[64] Viewed from this perspective, our diplomatic "success" in Turkey was at best a "Pyrrhic" victory.

Much the same process has occurred with cocaine and marijuana. Prior to 1970, substantially all U.S. cocaine came from coca leaves grown in the mountains of Colombia. Thereafter, coca harvesting spread to the mountains of Bolivia and Peru. In 1984, the DEA reported that coca harvesting had now spread further—to the mountains of Brazil, Ecuador, and Venezuela.[65]

Prior to 1970, an estimated 80 percent of all U.S. marijuana came from Mexico. That country, under U.S. prodding, is waging intensive war on its marijuana growers, and so Mexico now shares the U.S. marijuana market with Belize, Brazil, Costa Rica, Columbia, Indonesia, Jamaica, Laos, Nigeria, Panama, Thailand, Venezuela, and perhaps other countries as well.[66]

Here are some piquant details of other diplomatic "successes," culled from the latest (1984) DEA and NNICC intelligence estimates:

Marijuana in Jamaica.[67] In 1983, Jamaican growers had an estimated 4,600 acres of marijuana under cultivation. Government agents, prodded by the U.S., destroyed crops grown on nearly one-fifth of that acreage. This form of crop control prevented over-production, but it did not prevent Jamaican growers from supplying an estimated 14 percent of the marijuana imported into the United States during the year. Jamaica remained second only to Colombia in tons of marijuana exported to the U.S.

Marijuana in Belize.[68] This is a small country which produces two marijuana crops a year. The DEA reports: "The Belizean government eradicated about 95 percent of the fall 1983 crop, significantly reducing the amount available for export. . . . The Belize Defense Force and National Police were mobilized to provide ground support to aerial spraying operations, over 3,000 cannabis production sites were destroyed."

By the spring of 1984, however, conditions had changed. There was a national Belizean election in 1984, and the aerial spraying program was, of course, unpopular not only among marijuana growers, but also among their neighbors who feared the herbicides being sprayed and among tradespeople dependent on the patronage of marijuana growers. To quote the DEA again, "the Belizean government declined to risk the adverse political effects of conducting an aerial spray operation during the 1984 election year." So the whole crop was safely marketed and shipped to the U.S.

Marijuana in Mexico.[69] According to the DEA, "the Government of Mexico continued to give high priority to cannabis eradication; about 6,500 acres of cannabis were destroyed in 1983, more than tripling the amount destroyed in 1982." The destruction was accomplished, as in Belize, by the aerial spraying of herbicides. Despite the vastly increased spraying, however, "approximately 1,300 tons of Mexican marijuana was available for distribution in the United States in 1983, compared to 750 tons in 1982."

The herbicide spraying also profoundly altered the pattern of marijuana production—in Mexico as in other countries. Traditionally, marijuana culture was concentrated in three Mexican states; by 1983, it had spread to three additional states, with smaller amounts being produced in every other Mexican state. In 1982, marijuana was being grown on large plots of 100 acres or so—easy targets for aerial spraying. By 1983, these large plantations had disappeared; "most cannabis fields consisted of smaller open areas," harder to spot and to spray from the air. Some of the 1983 plots "used modern irrigation and cultivation techniques" to increase the yield per acre and thus make it possible to meet the U.S. demand with fewer acres of marijuana. Despite the intensified marijuana eradication program, "Mexico expanded its share of the U.S. marijuana supply from six percent in 1982 to nine percent in 1983; it remained third among foreign exporters."

Cocaine Processing in Colombia.[70] Traditionally, Colombia not only cultivated coca bushes on a large scale, but also processed the coca leaves grown there and grown in neighboring countries as well. U.S. diplomatic efforts were successful in persuading the Colombian government to make war on cocaine processing. "In late 1982," says a NNICC report, "the Colombian government took steps to curtail the availability of essential chemicals needed to process cocaine. The Colombian Attorney General issued instructions to place ether, acetone, and sulphuric acid on a list of restricted imported items. . . . As a result of these import restrictions neither ether nor potassium permanganate was imported legally into Colombia in 1983." In addition, Colombian law enforcement authorities seized and destroyed 100 cocaine processing laboratories during the year.

As a result, Peruvian and Bolivian traffickers began to process their own cocaine instead of shipping the leaves to Colombia for processing. Cocaine processing labs were also established in Argentina, Chile, Costa Rica, and even in the United States. "In late 1982, a cocaine conversion laboratory was seized and four Peruvians were arrested in Beverly Hills, California."

In 1984, 22 cocaine labs were seized in the U.S., and during the first six months of 1985, 17 more were seized.[71] How many escaped seizure and continue to operate is not known.

CURBING U.S. MARIJUANA PRODUCTION

Though marijuana had for centuries grown wild in the U.S., almost all of our commercial black-market marijuana was imported prior to Operation Intercept in 1969. Then cultivation on a modest scale was reported in California.

The spraying of foreign marijuana fields with paraquat and other herbicides meant a bonanza for California growers, for U.S. marijuana smokers who had long preferred imported marijuana now demanded domestic marijuana to avoid the adverse effects of herbicide residues. Thus, the foreign herbicide spraying program became in effect a kind of farm-aid program, helping U.S. marijuana growers capture a larger share of the market. Foreign observers were quick to note that, while U.S. diplomats were urging *them* to spray paraquat and other herbicides on *their* marijuana, California marijuana crops remained unsullied. So an herbicide spraying program was launched in California, too.

One effect, as might be expected, was to decentralize production. Commercial marijuana-growing spread from California to nearby states and then across the country. The government's herbicide-spraying program followed suit. In 1982, 40 states participated in the DEA marijuana-spraying program, with spraying scheduled for 47 states in 1984, and all 50 states in 1985.[72]

The 1983 NNICC report boasted, ''As a result of the DEA's Domestic Eradication Program, almost 3.8 million marijuana plants were destroyed in the United States in 1983, a nearly 50-percent increase over the previous year. Arrests at cultivation sites increased about 70 percent.''[73]

The same NNICC report also noted, however, how U.S. marijuana growers were adapting to the spraying program: ''Cultivation of domestic cannabis became more sophisticated and widespread in 1983. There was increased use of commercial-scale greenhouses, indoor gardening, and hydroponic facilities to produce cannabis. (Hydroponics is the practice of cultivating plants in a solution of nutrients rather than soil.) Growers appeared to be moving their cultivation indoors to avoid detection and destruction by law enforcement agencies.''[74]

There was also a shift from ordinary marijuana to a much more potent variety of marijuana called sinsemilla; indeed, the average potency for U.S.-grown marijuana nearly doubled between 1979 and 1983,[75] which meant that one acre in 1983 did the work of two 1979 acres. The DEA described in some detail an example of the new cultivation technique:

> In August 1983, a hydroponic marijuana laboratory was seized in Cleveland, Ohio. The laboratory was housed on three floors of a commercial foundry building in an industrial area of the city. The facility consisted of three sinsemilla growing levels with a constant flowing nutrient system piped throughout from a 600-gallon nutrient tank. One floor was used as a starter area and equipped with fluorescent lighting. The other two levels

> were for maturing plants and contained about 50 high-intensity lights. Two floors of marijuana, totalling over 400 plants, dried marijuana from drying rooms, several trash bags of manicured marijuana, and $50,000 worth of equipment were seized at the facility.[76]

Such a "marijuana lab" can yield three crops a year, totalling 1,200 sinsemilla plants, with a *wholesale* value estimated by the DEA at $1,500 per plant, or a gross for the year of $1,800,000 from that abandoned Cleveland foundry building. It is unlikely that a dearth of abandoned foundries, factories, or warehouses will limit sinsemilla production in the future.

THE FUTURE

It is possible, of course, that the DEA will enact some new technique of law enforcement more effective than the techniques relied on since the San Francisco opium-den ordinance of 1875, escalating the penalties, beefing up law enforcement budgets, sealing the borders, discouraging production overseas and at home. But the American system of illicit drug distribution also has some unplayed aces up its sleeve. For example:

1. Opium poppies were once grown commercially throughout the United States. A Massachusetts official reported in 1871 that,

> Opium has recently been made from white poppies, cultivated for the purpose, in Vermont, New Hampshire, and Connecticut, the annual production being estimated in hundreds of pounds. . . . Opium has also been brought here from Florida and Louisiana, while comparatively large quantities are regularly sent east from California and Arizona, where its cultivation is becoming an important branch of industry, ten acres of poppies being said to yield, in Arizona, 1,200 pounds of opium.[77]

There is no reason why, if heroin imports are successfully curtailed hereafter, this domestic cultivation of opium poppies cannot be resumed, perhaps hydroponically, indoors.[78]

2. Coca bushes are now cultivated almost exclusively in the

Andes Mountains. There is no botanical reason why, if imports are successfully curtailed hereafter, the bushes cannot also be cultivated in the Rocky Mountains and the Appalachians.

3. Finally, chemists are quite capable of synthesizing heroin, cocaine, and the active principle in marijuana (THC), just as they now synthesize LSD and the amphetamines in clandestine U.S. laboratories.

For these and other reasons, I conclude that the future of law enforcement as a method of drug control looks as bleak as its past. Nor am I alone in this view. On July 5, 1985, the *New York Times* published an interview with John C. Lawn, who had just been appointed by President Reagan as Chief of the DEA. Administrator Lawn, the *Times* explained, had worked in the FBI from 1967 to 1982. "Through those years, he said, he had approached law enforcement with the view that 'if you put sufficient resources into a case, eventually you are going to solve it.'" Then, in 1982, he became Assistant Director of the DEA. He came to his new job "convinced that the same philosophy would work against drugs. Like others before, he believed that 'with sufficient resources, the drug problem could be addressed and reversed with law enforcement alone.'"[79]

But three years at the DEA taught him his error. "I can't go out and say that with added resources the DEA is going to go out and solve the drug problem," President Reagan's DEA Administrator told Joel Brinkley of the *Times* in 1985, "because we aren't. The problem is greater than law enforcement is able to cope with."

He then went on to cite for the *Times* correspondent some of the same evidence of DEA failure that I have cited above; indeed, as the footnotes show, some of the evidence of failure I cite came from Lawn's interview with Brinkley.

Over the last 20 years, the same interview continued, the DEA and its predecessors "have tried a succession of new approaches: special operations, new organizations, and equipment. But whatever they have tried, the drug traffickers have quickly adapted, and the trafficking has gone on, seemingly unabated." In short, it is impossible to beat the free-enterprise system of illicit drug production and distribution.

With respect to the future, Brinkley wrote, "Mr. Lawn believes that the statistics will not improve until there is a 'perceptible change' in attitudes of the public about using drugs. 'We've got to put more emphasis on the demand side, on education,' he said.''[80]

I have no better suggestion.

REFERENCES

1. Terry, C. E., & Pellens, M. (1928), *The Opium Problem*, New York: Committee on Drug Addictions, Bureau of Social Hygiene, Inc., reprinted (1970) by Patterson Smith Publishing Corp., Montclair, N.J.
2. Howe, H. S. (1955), in *New York State Journal of Medicine* 55: 341–348.
3. Kane, H. H. (1882), *Opium Smoking in America and China*, p. 73.
4. Terry & Pellens (1928).
5. Brecher, E. M., and the Editors of Consumer Reports (1972), *Licit and Illicit Drugs: The Consumers Union Report on Narcotics, Stimulants, Depressants, Inhalants, Hallucinogens, and Marijuana—Including Caffeine, Nicotine, and Alcohol*. Boston: Little, Brown.
6. U.S. Department of Justice, Drug Enforcement Administration (1984), *DEA Quarterly Intelligence Trends*, Vol. 2. Washington, D.C.
7. National Narcotics Intelligence Consumers Committee (1983), *NNICC Narcotics Intelligence Estimate*. Washington, D.C.
8. Brecher et al. (1972), p. 46.
9. Kane (1882), p. 73.
10. *Idem*.
11. Kolb, L., & DuMez, A. G. (1924). *The Prevalence and Trend of Drug Addiction in the United States and Factors Influencing It*. U.S. Public Health Service Reprint No. 924. Washington, D.C.: U.S. Government Printing Office. p. 14.
12. Public Law No. 221, 60th Congress, approved February 9, 1909.
13. Anslinger, H. J., & Tompkins, W. F. (1930). *The Traffic in Narcotics*. New York: Funk & Wagnalls, p. 54.
14. Kolb, L. (1925), in *Mental Hygiene*, 9:719–720.
15. Quoted in Blum, R., et al. (1968), *Utopiates*. New York: Atherton Press, p. 205.
16. Brecher et al. (1972), pp. 48–49.
17. Public Law No. 223, 63rd Congress, approved December 17, 1914.
18. *Idem*.
19. Brecher et al. (1972), pp. 49–50.
20. *New York Medical Journal* (1915), 102:1014.
21. *American Medicine* (1915), 10(U.S.): 799–800.
22. Campbell, H. (1922), in *British Journal of Inebriety*, 20:147.
23. Brecher et al. (1972), p. 56.
24. Brecher et al. (1972), pp. 56–58.
25. Clemency application, Gilbert Morazargoza to Attorney General Robert F. Kennedy, January 18, 1962.
26. Brecher et al. (1972), pp. 58–59.
27. Kolb & DuMez (1924).
28. NNICC (1983), p. 35.
29. Brecher et al. (1972), pp. 90–100.
30. Brecher et al. (1972), p. 92.
31. Arthur D. Little, Inc. (1967), *Drug Abuse and Law Enforcement*, Tables I–IV, pp. 1–4.
32. *Idem*.

33. Brecher et al. (1972), pp. 90–100.
34. *Ibid.*, p. 92.
35. *ibid.*, pp. 92–93.
36. *Ibid.*, pp. 93–94.
37. *Ibid.*, p. 304.
38. *Ibid.*, p. 278.
39. *Ibid.*, p. 280.
40. *Ibid.*, pp. 281–283; p. 302.
41. *Idem.*
42. *New York Times*, February 1, 1970.
43. *Idem.*
44. Brecher et al. (1972), pp. 302–303.
45. Interview with DEA Administrator John C. Lawn, *New York Times*, July 5, 1985.
46. Brecher et al. (1972), pp. 403–405.
47. Brecher et al. (1972), pp. 410–412.
48. Brecher et al. (1972), p. 413.
49. *Journal of the American Medical Association* (1937), 108:1543.
50. *Congressional Record*, January 20, 1970, pp. S 240–245.
51. NNICC (1983), p. 7.
52. Brecher et al. (1972), p. 434–450.
53. *New York Times*, September 22, 1969.
54. *Idem.*
55. Associated Press dispatch in *New York Daily News*, September 29, 1969.
56. Robert Lindsey in the *New York Times*, November 30, 1971.
57. McGlothin, W., Jamison, K., & Rosenblatt, S. (1970), in *Nature* (London), 228:1227–1229.
58. Brecher et al. (1972), pp. 443–450.
59. Brecher et al. (1972), pp. 436–440.
60. *New York Times*, October 10, 1969.
61. *New York Times*, September 25, 1969.
62. Brecher et al. (1972), p. 440.
63. Brecher et al. (1972), pp. 90–91.
64. DEA (1984), *Quarterly Intelligence Trends*, pp. 36–37.
65. DEA (1984), *Quarterly Intelligence Trends*, pp. 20–27.
66. DEA (1984), *Quarterly Intelligence Trends*, pp. 12–13.
67. DEA (1984), *Quarterly Intelligence Trends*, pp. 13–14; NNICC (1983), *Narcotics Intelligence Estimate*, pp. 10–11.
68. NNICC (1983), *Narcotics Intelligence Estimates*, pp. 11–12; DEA (1984), *Quarterly Intelligence Trends*, p. 15.
69. DEA (1984), *Quarterly Intelligence Trends*, pp. 14–15; NNICC (1983), *Narcotics Intelligence Estimate*, pp. 11.
70. DEA (1984), *Quarterly Intelligence Trends*, pp. 20–27; NNICC (1983), *Narcotics Intelligence Estimate*, pp. 19–25.
71. Interview with John C. Lawn, *New York Times*, July 5, 1985.
72. *Idem.*
73. NNICC (1983), *Narcotics Intelligence Estimate*, p. 9.
74. *Ibid.*, p. 8.
75. NNICC (1983), *Narcotics Intelligence Estimate*, p. 3.
76. DEA (1984), *Quarterly Intelligence Trends*, p. 10.
77. Massachusetts State Board of Health (1870), *Annual Report*.
78. State's Attorney Philip H. White of Orleans County, Vermont, reported in September, 1985, that police had found 2,000 opium poppies growing in the northern Vermont town of West Charleston. Many of the poppy pods had already been slit to extract the raw opium. Previously, Mr. White noted, it was believed that opium was not being grown in the United

States, but reports of opium poppy cultivation had recently come in from Michigan, California, and Washington state, as well as Vermont (*New York Times*, September 22, 1985, p. 55).

79. Interview with John C. Lawn, *New York Times*, July 5, 1985.

80. *Idem*.

The Deviance Model of Drug-Taking Behavior: A Critique

Charles Winick, Ph.D.

ABSTRACT. The deviance model has become the most widely accepted American approach to explain nonprescription use of psychoactive drugs. Little attention, however, has been given to the evaluation of its utility and current relevance to account for the use and abuse of scheduled drugs. This article examines the deviance model and explores some of the implications that result from its employment. A major problem with the deviance model is that it does not account for changes in patterns of drug use over time and changes in attitude toward drugs that accompany current trends in drug use. The model also does not account for different motives for drug use and among different classes or types of drug users. These and other issues are discussed and a recommendation is provided to help make the deviance model more responsive to different forms of drug-taking behavior.

The most widely accepted American approach to the description of drug-taking behavior, other than the use of prescription drugs under the supervision of a physician, is a deviance model. This model applies to drug use, dependence, misuse, and abuse. Dependence involves a physical and/or psychological reliance on a substance; misuse includes unsupervised use of prescription drugs or use of other substances on a self-directed basis; and abuse refers to patterns of use for the purpose of psychoactive effects or the use of illegal substances in a manner that may be harmful to the individual. All of these terms involve the ascription of deviance to the drug-taking behavior.

The deviance model of drug-taking has been widely accepted for

Charles Winick is with the Department of Sociology, CUNY Graduate Center, 33 West 42 Street, New York, NY 10036-8099.

so long that little attention has been given to its utility and current relevance. This article will examine the model and explore some implications of its employment.

The deviance model is undergirded by legal and international controls. Drug-taking outside of medical supervision is largely illegal, because even regulated licit prescription substances may only be possessed by someone who has a physician's prescription to do so. Some widely used illicit substances, such as heroin, have no current medical use and are classified in Schedule I by the U.S. Drug Enforcement Administration, indicating highest potential for abuse. The United States ratified the 1961 Single Convention on Narcotic Drugs in 1967 and thus agreed to participate in international regulation of psychoactive substances.

Drug use for purposes of self-directed mood modification is regularly presented as deviant behavior in sociology and social problems textbooks (e.g., Akers, 1985; Rusing, 1969; Henslin & Light, 1983) and federal government policy formulations (Secretary of Health & Human Services, 1984). The lead federal agency concerned with such matters is called the National Institute on Drug *Abuse*, a title that clearly communicates aberrant behavior. The World Health Organization recommendation that the less evaluative term "dependence" be used was never favorably received here (Eddy et al., 1965).

Looking at the major theories on the genesis and continuation of drug abuse, what proportion are based on a deviance model? The National Institute of Drug Abuse published a volume summarizing the 43 leading theories culled from a broad range of academic disciplines (Lettieri et al., 1980). Of these theories, 26 clearly involved a significant component of drug use as deviant, "pariah," or disapproved behavior.

The American Psychiatric Association (1980), which had previously adopted a relatively neutral stance with respect to drug-taking, positioned substance abuse as a mental disorder in the latest edition of its Diagnostic and Statistical Manual. Nineteen possible substance use disorders are listed in the manual.

Presentations of drug-taking in entertainment and news media regularly present the activity as deviant (Winick, 1974a). The many surveys of incidence and prevalence of drug use similarly report it as aberrant behavior.

SURVEY AND OTHER PREVALENCE DATA

When we look at any deviant activity or social problem, a logical question to ask is: How many people are involved in the activity? The National Survey on Drug Abuse in American households, the University of Michigan Monitoring the Future study of high school seniors, and surveys of many special groups provide current information on the incidence and prevalence of drug-taking. The most insistent type of data that could be cited toward a normative rather than a deviant model of drug-taking is provided by a large body of survey information on the use of mood-modifying substances by the general population and by many of its subgroups, notably young people. Surveys uniformly indicate that by the late 1970s, drug-taking had penetrated all levels of American society, raising the question of how so widespread a phenomenon can be considered to be deviant. Marihuana and cocaine, the leading recreational drugs, provide relevant examples.

Between 1965 and 1970 the proportion of college students who had used marihuana rose from 10 percent to 42 percent. By the end of the 1970s, two-thirds of young American adults had tried marihuana (Radosevich et al., 1980). Not only were millions of ordinary Americans smoking marihuana, but some famous American cultural icons were also doing so. Superstar pop singer John Denver and actress Mary Tyler Moore, exemplars of wholesome American living, admitted that they smoked marihuana (Anderson, 1981).

Cocaine, once a very expensive and relatively inaccessible drug, had been used by one out of every six high school seniors in 1983 (O'Malley, Johnston, & Bachman, 1985). Among young adults aged 18 to 25, 28 percent were reported in the most recent national household survey (Abelson & Miller, 1985) to have taken cocaine. Other stimulants, according to the National Survey on Drug Abuse, had been taken by 18 percent of young adults (Miller et al., 1983).

Anecdotal information on celebrities provides another dimension of use. A number of famous persons publicly admitted their use of cocaine for mood-modifying purposes in the 1980s. The country's most successful movie actor in the early part of the decade, Richard Pryor, achieved much fame by his open discussion of cocaine use. At a Pittsburgh trial in September 1985, a number of the most famous professional baseball players in the country admitted their purchase and regular use of cocaine. Celebrities, in general, do not seem to be prosecuted for their possession of cocaine. At the 1983 Hollywood Academy Awards ceremony, the evening's most enthusiastic applause was given to host Johnny Carson in his discussion of the financial success of the different Hollywood organizations. He noted that in the previous year, the most money had been made by "Colombia, the country, not the studio." The millions of people in the television audience presumably understood the reference.

While cocaine use by the famous regularly gets into the headlines, ordinary people all over America were taking cocaine on a routine basis. In New York City, studies of working-class persons found cocaine rapidly becoming the most widely used recreational drug (Winick, 1985); it ranked sixth in incidence and was the drug of choice of three percent of the clients of a large and representative employee assistance program in 1980, but 21 percent favored it by 1984, making it the most popular substance. The new popularity of cocaine probably derives from its more favorable image among the general public and a simultaneous decrease in the cost and increase in availability of the drug.

During the late 1970s, relatively high levels of use were also reported in national surveys for other drugs, such as stimulants, hallucinogens, inhalants, opioids, sedative-hypnotics, tranquilizers and depressants. Although levels of most forms of drug-taking have declined somewhat in the early 1980s, they are nevertheless still high.

When a small number of people are involved in an activity such as drug-taking behavior, it is reasonable to expect that they will differ significantly, in terms of demographic and socioeconomic characteristics, from the general population. For two decades prior to the 1960s there was wide acceptance of the figure of 60,000 heroin addicts in the United States. Today, the figure of 500,000 heroin addicts had been widely accepted. It was not surprising that while the 60,000 addicts in the 1950s had clearly identifiable characteristics, today's 500,000 addicts have fewer such characteristics, but they can still be differentiated from the other 240,000,000 Americans.

However, when we look at the many millions of people using marihuana or cocaine relatively frequently for social-recreational purposes, they represent so large a proportion of the population that it is no longer possible to differentiate social-structural characteristics of the users from those of the general population.

Similar considerations apply to the users of licit psychotropic substances. One of the few post-1960s household studies designed to document whether there were measurable sociodemographic differences between adults who were and who were not users of psychotropic substances found no such differences. In this national household probability sample survey of adults aged 18 to 55, conducted specifically to identify sociological dimensions of sedative-hypnotic psychotropic drug use, Borgatta (1974) reported no significant differences between users and nonusers. Additional analyses conducted of interpersonal and coping variables were similarly "disappointing" in failing to yield consistent relationships with use. One implication of the study is that sedative-hypnotic drug use, involving over one-sixth of the adult population, is so normative in this country that a study carefully designed to identify characteristics of the user subgroups was unable to do so. If an activity is engaged in by a large proportion of the population and if its practitioners have no characteristics that distinguish them from the general population, how deviant can the activity be?

MARIHUANA USE AS A DEVIANT ACTIVITY

Marihuana, which has been the most widely used social-recreational drug, has become the focus of a significant effort to change the drug's connotations of deviance. One contributor to the early view of marihuana use as a deviant activity was Becker's (1953) influential analysis of how people become users of the substance. Perhaps as important as the social learning theory of drug use, which Becker proposed, was his association of marihuana use with dance musicians, who were often perceived, at the time, to be members of a deviant group. Several reports subsequently documented the extent to which the parallel pariah status of marihuana and jazz influenced both the music and the public perceptions of marihuana (Winick, 1961, 1962a). Marihuana use was also linked with Mexican immigrants and urban ghetto residents.

Ever since these early reports, marihuana and other drug use have been linked with social discontent, political alienation, and similar labels (Clarke & Levine, 1971). During the 1960s and 1970s, smoking marihuana was often associated with opposition to the Vietnam war and was otherwise perceived to be a symbol of rebellion and countercultural thinking (Suchman, 1968).

In spite of such connotations of marihuana as a vehicle of rebellion in popular culture, there have been many legal, official, and professional moves toward recognizing recreational use of marijuana as a nondeviant activity. Starting in 1973 with Oregon, ten other states with about one-third of the country's population (Alaska, Maine, Colorado, California, Ohio, Minnesota, Mississippi, New York, North Carolina and Nebraska) passed laws decriminalizing marihuana in the next few years.

The conservative Commission on Marihuana and Drug Abuse (1973), appointed by President Nixon, recommended decriminalization of marihuana possession. In the same year a World Health Organization study group made a similar proposal.

In 1972, the LeDain Commission in Canada had recommended that marihuana possession be legalized and the American Medical Association (AMA) urged that criminal penalties for possession of small amounts of marihuana be eliminated. Five years later, the AMA joined the American Bar Association in proposing decriminalization.

One reason for the decriminalization movement was that following the anti-marihuana laws to their logical conclusions could have led to a collapse of the criminal justice system under the weight of an enormous number of prosecutions. In 1977, for example, there were 458,000 people arrested for violation of state laws against possession of marihuana. Processing these cases through the procedures of arraignment, indictment, trial, sentencing, probation, prison, and parole, could have placed an impossible burden on the criminal justice system.

The decriminalization statutes did ease the strain on the system. The number of arrests for possession of marihuana in California, for example, dropped from 88,000 in 1975 to 10,000 in 1976, the first year of decriminalization. The state saved over $25 million a year in police and court costs.

A survey conducted in Oregon, after passage of the decriminalization law, concluded that there was no significant increase in marihuana use and most residents of the state approved the law. The percentage of adults who had ever used marihuana increased from nineteen to twenty-five percent, from 1974 to 1977, and current users advanced from nine to ten percent in the same period (Drug Abuse Council, 1978).

Since Nebraska passed its decriminalization bill in 1978, no other state has done so. This is probably not because the issue is politically hazardous, inasmuch as no politician who supported decriminalization failed to win re-election or election in 1976, when the issue was being actively discussed. Several larger political and social developments changed the public and legislative perception of marihuana in the late 1970s.

The American Council on Marihuana was started in 1979 to educate the country about the hazards of marihuana. Its message carried special weight because the Council's president was Dr. Robert I. DuPont, who had been the first director of the National Institute of Drug Abuse, and who had previously recommended decriminalization. Around the same time, Families in Action, in Atlanta, became the leader in what became a major national parents' movement against teenage drug abuse and, more specifically, against marihuana. The parents' movement, spurred by White House support and First Lady Nancy Reagan's stress on the family as the bulwark against drug abuse, has flourished. Former President Carter's effort to repeal the federal laws against marihuana possession was associated with other failures of his administration and was denounced by President Reagan's drug program leaders.

SOME APPROACHES TO DRUG-TAKING AS A NONDEVIANT ACTIVITY

An early contributor to the view that the deviance model of drug taking was inappropriate was sociologist Alfred R. Lindesmith (1947), who argued that narcotic drugs were benign and that federal and local enforcement policies had created an artificial criminal subculture. A joint committee of the American Medical Association and the American Bar Association (1964) came to a somewhat similar conclusion. Around the same time, the identification of narcotics and other drug abuse as a noteworthy example of victimless crime raised questions about the wisdom of our laws restricting access to mood-modifying substances (Schur, 1965).

On another level, the deviance approach to the explanation of drug use has been challenged by several influential social problem theorists. The symbolic interaction approach called attention to social and symbolic meanings of alcohol and drug use, with nonuse having connotations of the desirable and use regarded as antisocial (Gusfield, 1963). Conflict theorists showed how the criminalization of drug use maintains the status quo and absorbs the energies of potential revolutionaries (Karmen, 1974; Helmer, 1975). Functional theory pointed to the role played by criminalization of drug use in maintenance of ghetto economies and careers for large numbers of bureaucrats and service providers (Casey & Preble, 1974; Regush, 1971). Lemert's (1967) notion of secondary deviance, as part of his exposition of labeling theory, argued that laws and policy determine drug users' contacts with criminals and other deviants. Social network, exchange, and general systems theory have been integrated to explain how professionals' status and rewards, in the early 1970s, flourished via "trafficking" in information on drugs or drug users or receiving and making referrals of young drug users to or from members of twelve professions (Beniger, 1983). Revisionist theory in political science questioned the validity of official information on the nature and dimensions of the country's drug problem (Epstein, 1977).

Another challenge to the traditional American approach to drug abuse as deviance is represented by the introduction of the methadone maintenance approach to the treatment of heroin addiction in the 1960s, and its widespread acceptance since then. Any form of pharmacotherapy had previously been vigorously opposed by federal authorities concerned with policy toward heroin addiction. Only the 1962 retirement of Commissioner Harry J. Anslinger of the Federal Bureau of Narcotics made possible the climate of opinion in which heroin addicts could receive methadone, a substitute opioid that enabled them to function. The introduction of methadone maintenance and its vast expansion in the 1970s involved acceptance of the notion that there are many people whose use of a dependence-provoking drug is necessary for their adaptation to social living.

The 1960s and 1970s also witnessed the enormous attention given to scientists who urged the positive contributions of psychedelic drugs (Weil, 1972). Psychologist Timothy Leary achieved great media and scientific attention by his pronouncements on "turning on" via drugs. From 1963 to 1968 millions of middle-class youths accepted the notion that drugs represented a socially desirable way to expand one's consciousness.

All of these developments contributed to calling into question the traditional deviance model of drug-taking behavior.

COMPLEXITIES IN CLASSIFICATION OF DRUG USE PURPOSES

Any effort to evaluate the relative merit of the deviance model of drug use must consider the many kinds of reasons for which people take psychoactive drugs. People may begin taking some drugs for benign purposes or under a physician's supervision and gradually escalate their use, for reasons that they could not predict. Former First Lady Betty Ford began taking analgesics for relief of pain stemming from arthritis and a pinched nerve and found herself in a condition of iatrogenic sedativism. The same situation developed with the prominent television producer Barbara Gordon (1980). How far should a person go in terms of enduring pain before engaging in self-medication? If a physician establishes drug use as the recommended approach to handling symptoms, what can the patient do to protect himself or herself from the physician's enthusiastic reliance on pharmacotherapy? When the larger culture provides such support for the notion of using chemicals to facilitate coping behavior, how can the user know when such use is inappropriate?

The differences between taking drugs for medical reasons and for such social recreational purposes as feeling better or different are becoming substantially blurred. Three-tenths of all prescriptions are written for psychoactive drugs, which will presumably also make the patient feel better or different. It is difficult to distinguish medical from recreational reasons, especially since self-medication is a dominant method of health care in the United States, with physicians probably seeing only a fourth to a third of the persons with illnesses, injuries, or other symptoms (Hughes & Brewin, 1979). Some 350,000 products are sold over the counter (OTC) for self-medication in this country. Questions are being raised about the decision to classify specific kinds of self-medication as drug abuse but to permit and encourage other types of medicating oneself as normal drug use.

Approximately one-tenth of American adults regularly take products sold over the counter for encouragement of sleep, relief of pain or tension or anxiety, or for the easing of other symptoms via sedative-hypnotic substances. Undoubtedly, many Americans also take illicit substances for similar purposes. The OTC product users are presumably not engaging in deviant behavior but the latter group would have to be classified as deviant.

Probably the most sustained effort to view psychoactive drug taking as normative has been mounted by Zinberg (1984), who has discussed the importance of identifying the occasional, moderate, noncompulsive, and circumstantial uses of chemical substances. Although there is general acceptance of the idea that a person may take alcohol in a noncompulsive manner over a lifetime, there is little support for the notion that other drugs may be taken in a similarly nonabusive manner. There is a tendency to regard use of such drugs as a gateway or transition to "hard" use of other substances. The person who only takes "hard" or "soft" drugs at a rock concert or in other specific social situations, or on a controlled or noncompulsive basis, does not figure significantly in user typologies or policy pronouncements.

A related consideration is that much drug taking is self-limiting in terms of time. The notion that drug dependence lasts for many years has been challenged by a number of studies. Winick (1962b) suggested, even in the case of heroin, that there is a very high negative correlation of use with age, and that most addicts mature out of their addiction without treatment. Another way of expressing this is to identify the points in the life cycle at which heroin use is most likely to begin and end (Winick, 1964, 1974b). Not only heroin but most recreational drug use peaks in the early 20s, remains at high levels through the mid-20s, and drops substantially thereafter (Cisin et al., 1983). Linking drug-taking activities with the life cycle should make it easier to understand their situational dimensions and helps to position such activities as less likely to be defined as deviant.

SOME IMPLICATIONS OF A NONDEVIANCE MODEL OF DRUG-TAKING FOR SURVEYS

Consideration of a nondeviance model of drug-taking would have direct implications for surveys. The many regular surveys of incidence and prevalence are very influential. The results of such surveys help in policy formation, and are widely used by legislators to influence program direction.

Since so much energy is devoted to developing surveys of drug use, it would seem simple to include questions on the functions served by the drugs, the situations in which and persons with whom they are used, and on the life styles of the respondents, in addition to the usual questions on frequency of use. Information on drug situations, functions, leisure and life styles, would enormously increase our understanding of drug-taking and the context in which it occurs. We can hypothesize that the situations of use and functions served by drugs would reflect different life epochs. There has been an enormous concentration on drug habits of people under 25, but less attention has been paid to the connotations and symbolic dimensions of drug use by older persons.

A number of typologies of drug use already exist and could be incorporated into ongoing surveys. Since practically all significant surveys are funded either by the National Institute of Drug Abuse or by one of the designated single state agencies, it would be relatively easy to encourage incorporation of such questions.

Chein (1965) proposed a four-way typology of compulsive drug use:

1. strong craving for the substance with little involvement with a subculture;
2. strong involvement with a subculture but relatively little craving;
3. strongly influenced by both craving and personal involvement; and
4. neither strongly craving nor personally involved.

A related typology was proposed by Brotman and Freedman (1969):

1. conformists who live conventionally with little involvement in crime;
2. hustlers who are highly involved in crime but not in conventional life;
3. two worlders who are highly involved in both areas of life; and
4. those uninvolved in either area.

Davis and Munoz (1968) made a distinction between Appolonian "heads" who use drugs to achieve insight and expand their sensibility and "freaks" who use them in order to achieve hedonistic satisfaction.

Another typology classifies the substance's salience to its users in four categories: (1) experimenters whose use is episodic; (2) social/recreational users with whom drug use is part of other activities and is situational/occasional; (3) committed users with whom the substance is central to the person's life; and (4) dysfunctional users with whom the substance dominates the person's life (Chambers, 1974). A related approach involves classifying drugs in terms of whether they complement life, cause transient problems, or cause major and continuing problems (Ray, 1978). Not only have a number of other scholars proposed typologies that include a range of different relationships to drugs, but a Presidential commission (Commission on Marihuana and Drug Abuse, 1972), an expert task force for another Presidential commission (Liaison Panel on Psychoactive Drug Use/Misuse, 1980), and a cabinet level federal government committee (Domestic Council Drug Abuse Task Force, 1975) have made similar recommendations. Including such typology-oriented questions in surveys would greatly improve the utility of the surveys.

Drug-taking tends to be perceived as an either/or phenomenon in surveys. Substances that are ingested are presumed to be taken for abuse purposes in most surveys. In reality, a respondent might be taking one prescription drug for treatment of symptoms and under the supervision of a physician, trying an OTC or other prescription product for self-medication purposes, using another OTC product for purposes of relaxation, or ingesting an illicit drug in a social situation in order not to appear to be a deviant in that situation. Each of these situations involves a different kind of relationship to the substance, but in current survey methodology, each incident of use has equal weight. On Monday, the same drug that had served one function on Sunday could be taken for the purpose of meeting different needs. An operationally defined typology of drug uses and functions is needed so that surveys, for the first time, can report the range and social context of the different patterns of drug use and relate them to specific subgroups in the population.

Amphetamines, for example, might be taken for a wide range of purposes: to lose weight, keep alert while driving a truck, assist in studying for an examination, or obtain a high. They could be ingested in a social situation or while the user is alone. They might have been acquired by prescription or through a friend. If obtained from a physician, the amphetamines may or may not be used for the purpose for which the prescription was written. The drug could be used by a student, truck driver, ghetto resident, musician, or unemployed person. All of these considerations enter into the decision to consider a specific incident of amphetamine use as a deviant activity.

No national surveys, however, ask questions on the purposes of or the reasons for or the social context of the use of a substance, with the recent exception of the University of Michigan Monitoring the Future survey, in which respondents were given a list of fifteen reasons, and asked, ‘‘What have been the most important reasons for your taking ______?’’ (Johnston, Bachman, & O’Malley, 1984). The reasons included to ‘‘see what its like’’ (79.3 percent for cocaine and 64.6 percent for marihuana), ‘‘to have a good time with my friends’’ (49.8 and 64.5 percent, respectively), ‘‘to relax, relieve tension’’ (22.5 and 41.8 percent, respectively).

In view of the wide range of substances that are ingested for mood-modifying purposes and the possibility that the same mood goal of the user might be achieved by a range of products, licit and illicit, it is important that surveys ask about all relevant products. For example, the National Survey on Drug Abuse, which is the major contributor to policy and which has been conducted regularly in American households since 1971, does not inquire about OTC drugs, although we know that billions of doses of such products are taken annually for mood-modifying purposes.

Society is most concerned about young people’s drug use in terms of their possible progression from beer or wine to abuse of various illicit drugs like heroin, via cigarettes or hard liquor, marihuana, and prescription drugs. The progression concept implicitly assumes that use of any of these substances is potentially deviant because it can lead to the next higher level of use. Such movement along the track of potential abuse seems especially likely if the respondent has a circle of friends who are drug users and involved in the sale and distribution of drugs (Clayton & Voss, 1982). One implication of this progression or gateway concept is that questions on friendships and drug sales ought to be included in all surveys.

Another area of questioning is indicated in the area of role strain or deprivation, since it is possible that persons who are experiencing role strain or deprivation are relatively likely to move toward compulsive and dysfunctional use of various substances (Winick, 1974b). It is relatively easy to determine the degree to which an individual is experiencing role strain or deprivation, and questions on these areas of possible conflict should be part of any inventory of attitudes and behavior related to mood-modifying substances. Such questions would help to flesh out user lifestyle profiles, along with other data on recreational activities, time budgets, and related subjects.

In view of the possible importance of the concept of controlled drug use in the elaboration of a nondeviance model, surveys could incorporate questions on the respondents' scheduling of the drug-taking activity and its positioning in the users' life space. Surveys typically ask about the frequency of use, e.g., "in the last twelve months but less than once a month," but seldom inquire about the details of use, whether it was over a weekend, or if it was a planned routinized activity, punctuated the day or week, was part of a larger leisure activity, and other circumstances of the set and setting.

AVERAGE, NORMAL, AND HEALTHY BEHAVIOR

If we are considering turning away from the deviance model of drug use, how ought the normative use of drugs be described? At the peak of the culture-personality movement a half century ago, Edwards (1934) differentiated four kinds of representative persons: (1) the average person ranks at the midpoint of the distribution; (2) the normal person is healthy and integrated and varies little from the average; (3) the adjusted individual is reasonably adapted to the environment and its demands; and (4) the effective person, whether adjusted or normal, accomplishes his/her purposes.

Wegrocki (1939) carefully considered different dimensions of cultural and statistical concepts of abnormality. Addressing pychological dimensions of behavior, he defined the quintessence of abnormality as the tendency to choose a type of reaction that represents an escape from a conflict-producing situation instead of facing the problem. Today we would probably broaden Wegrocki's definition of abnormality, although relatively few social scientists have addressed this issue. It would be possible to spell out the details of behavior that represent pathology in substantial detail.

Of course, just because large numbers of people engage in an activity, it is not necessarily normal. For example, the entire population of a community might have a cold, which would then become a statistically average situation in that region. But such a situation could not be described as being normal, since a condition of disease cannot be normal. It does not normalize drug-taking merely to describe the large numbers of people who are using these substances.

In Nazi Germany during the 1930s, the regnant ideology involved acceptance of the idea of racial inequalities, dominant and subordinant races, institutionalized murder of millions of people, using people as means rather than ends, perceiving the primary role of women to be breeders, and personality authoritarianism. Although such belief systems and behaviors were officially promoted and part of the corpus of what constituted German health and mental health, we could not accept such attitudes and behaviors as normal, even though they were widespread. Any behavior that is dysfunctional for oneself or harmful to oneself or others cannot be classified as normal, even if its incidence is high in terms of a "statisticorelative" formulation. A theory based on statistics of the individual's actual behavior, without delving into its meaning, is not acceptable.

The likelihood is that there are several different groups of drug users, for each of which drug-taking has different salience and relationships to their degree of functioning. We need to know the distribution of drug-using types, defined via representative critical incidents, before we can assess the relative utility of the deviance model of drug-taking which is currently the dominant paradigm. We can certainly speculate that there are millions of social-recreational drug users, or persons who take drugs for purposes of enhancing adaptation, who are otherwise functioning effectively in their personal, social, work, and family activities, but who do not appear to be adequately described in terms of the regnant deviance model and who could not operationally be defined as abnormal, maladjusted, or ineffective, in terms of Edwards' typology.

SOME IMPLICATIONS FOR PREVENTION AND TREATMENT

Reexamination of the deviance model of drug use would have significant implications for prevention and education programs. Disseminating information about substances, moralistic overtones, and affective and humanistic education have generally been ineffective. More recently, psychological inoculation and pressure resistance strategies appear to have had some preliminary success (Botvin, 1984). Even greater success could be obtained if prevention programs would present the range of possible relationships that young people could have to psychoactive substances and include training modules based on the realities of how psychoactive substances are actually used.

What implications for treatment would result from a reevaluation of the deviance model? Since the deviance model is still a predominant approach employed in the treatment community, there has been little experience in assessing drug use problems in terms of treatment strategy based on new models. Although the DSM-III employs different axes for diagnosis of substance dependence, general personality characteristics, and degree of impairment, just how such dimensions relate to each other in terms of treatment plans is not clear and has not been the subject of any significant body of clinical reports. It is certainly possible that for many kinds of nonsalient or controlled drug use, there is no need for treatment of any kind. It is also possible that the group therapy type of experience that is central to so many treatment approaches is irrelevant to many users.

SOME ANALOGUES

Scientific, public, and legal opinions have changed with respect to many other health and public issues. Many behaviors that were once seen to be deviant are viewed more acceptingly today. In the sexual arena, cohabitation and homosexuality are examples of situations that can be cited for their possible relevance to drug-taking today.

One possible analogue to the drug situation is provided by what used to be a criminal activity known as "lewd and open cohabitation," or a man and woman who were not married but lived together. The laws against this condition have, up to recently, been enforced with vigor. Today, such living arrangements have been institutionalized and are taken for granted. The Census Bureau now routinely recognizes this type of household in its tabulations, noting that the two million unmarried couples now living together represent three times the number doing so in 1970 (Study . . . , 1985). Laws against such "unmarried-married" are still on the books in some states and have never been declared unconstitutional. The penal codes have remained intact although the activity that was once condemned and illegal is now taken for granted and normative. Books on etiquette discuss how such couples should be introduced and the courts have upheld such living arrangements. Appellate courts have upheld the right of an unmarried couple to co-sign a lease for an apartment, although twenty years ago such cohabitation, in many states, would have been grounds for eviction.

Public and legal attitudes toward homosexuality have similarly changed in recent years, but the laws tend to have reflected the shift. America was the most homophobic country in the world (Gorer, 1964). Every state had laws against homosexual conduct between consenting adults. However, more than half the states have not repealed such laws, following the Model Penal Code of the American Law Institute (1962). The American Psychiatric Association, in 1975, conducted a poll of its members and found that a majority were opposed to classifying homosexuality as a psychiatric illness. The DSM-III does not classify it as a disease (American Psychiatric Association, 1980). One reason for this dramatic change was the realization that the laws against homosexual activity were not effective in discouraging the behavior. The landmark study by Kinsey and his associates had such enormous impact partly because of its documentation of the large numbers of men who had participated in homosexual behavior. But probably its most startling finding was that homosexuality was not an either/or category, and that men could be rated on a six-point scale on their comparative involvement in both heterosexuality and homosexuality. The analogy to the deviance model of drug-taking is particularly clear when we are told that "of the 40 or 50 percent of the male population which has homosexual experience, certainly a high proportion would not be considered psychopathic personalities on the basis of anything else in their histories" (Kinsey et al., 1948).

Similarly, there is a large proportion of drug takers who tend to be young, like the males who engage in homosexual behavior, but certainly a very small proportion would be considered deviant on the basis of anything else in their histories. Most drug takers, like most males who experiment with homosexuality, do not persist in the behavior into later life. Society has changed its attitude toward homosexuals but not toward drug takers.

DISCUSSION

There are several occasions when certain drugs shifted in status from being routinely accepted to becoming "pariah" and illegal. Up to passage of the Harrison Act in 1914, at least a million

Americans regularly took opioids in OTC preparations for relief of menstrual difficulties, pain, insomnia, and anxiety. The cocaine in coca leaves figured prominently in popular beverages, including Mariani's Coca Wine and Coca Cola, which were readily available and consumed by millions of Americans until they were regulated by the Harrison Act. In the case of both opioids and cocaine, persons using them outside of medical supervision were transformed into members of deviant and criminal groups after December, 1914. Marihuana was smoked by substantial numbers of people until the Marihuana Tax Act of 1937 subjected it to federal regulation, and its possession became a crime.

The criminal connotations that these legislative changes conveyed to the substances involved have carried over into the present. Another official action that contributed to the images of many substances is the Drug Enforcement Administration's assigning substances to specific Schedules in terms of the degree of their abuse liability. Marihuana, for example, is in Schedule I, or the most dangerous category. It is time to reexamine existing laws and DEA Schedules in terms of actual experience with the various substances in contributing to adverse reactions, illness, and other negative consequences, as documented in the Drug Abuse Warning Network (DAWN) reports.

The physical addiction properties of mood modifiers are becoming less important in the assessment of drug hazards, e.g., cocaine, and should be considered in any evaluation of the personal and social consequences of the use of each type of substance. We have enough data to determine what proportion of the users of each substance are likely to become casualties, and over what period of time. Yet the same linear model of use as abuse is applied to all substances with the exception of alcohol, regardless of the data.

Collection and integration of such data might lead to a reevaluation of the deviance model of drug taking. What is likely to emerge is a multimodal taxonomy of drug-taking behavior, which would differentiate between the person who takes substances compulsively, has a significant involvement in a criminal subculture, and for whom such drug-taking is salient, and the several other and much more numerous kinds of drug users. A convergence of theory and data seems to be suggesting the possible utility of reevaluating the deviance model in which, by a massive synecdoche, the negative and dysfunctional dimensions of drug-taking have long been presumed to represent all other kinds of relationships to mood-modifying substances.

REFERENCES

Abelson, H. I., and Miller, J. D., "A decade of trends in cocaine use in the household population" in N. J. Kozel and E. H. Adams (Eds.), *Cocaine Use In America*. Rockville: National Institute on Drug Abuse, 1985, 35–49.

Akers, R. L. *Deviant Behavior: A Social Learning Approach*. Belmont: Wadsworth, 1985, 107–125.

American Law Institute, *Model Penal Code*. Philadelphia: The Institute, 1962.

American Medical Association and American Bar Association. *Narcotic Addiction, Crime or Disease*? Bloomington: Indiana University Press, 1964.

American Psychiatric Association, *Diagnostic and Statistical Manual of Mental Disorders, III*. Washington: The Association, 1980.

Anderson, P. *High in America*. New York: Viking, 1981.

Becker, H. S. Becoming a marihuana user. *American Journal of Sociology*, 39, 1953, 235–242.

Beniger, J. R. *Trafficking in Drug Users: Professional Exchange Networks in the Control of Deviance*. New York: Cambridge University Press, 1983.

Borgatta, E. Psychotropic drug use in American families, in C. Winick (Ed.), *Sociological Aspects of Drug Dependence*. Cleveland: CRC Press, 1974, 111–125.

Botvin, Prevention research, in Secretary of Health and Human Services (Ed.), *Drug Abuse and Drug Abuse Research*. Washington: U.S. Department of Health and Human Services, 1984, 35–52.

Brotman, R., and Freedman, A. M. *A Community Mental Health Approach to Addiction*. Washington: Government Printing Office, 1969.

Casey, J. J., and Preble, E. Narcotic addiction and crime, in C. Winick (Ed.) *Sociological Aspects of Drug Dependence*. Cleveland: CRC Press, 1974, 283–308.

Chambers, C. D. Speculations on a behavior progression typology of pleasure-seeking drug use, in C. Winick (Ed.) *Sociological Aspects of Drug Dependence*. Cleveland: CRC Press, 1974, 283–308.

Chein, I., et al. *The Road to H*. New York: Basic Books, 1965.

Cisin, I., et al. *The National Household Survey on Drug Abuse*. Rockville: National Institute on Drug Abuse, 1983.

Clarke, J. W., and Levine, E. L. Marihuana use, social discontent and political alienation. *American Political Science Review*, 1971, 65, 120–130.

Clayton, R. R., and Voss, H. L. Marihuana and cocaine: the causal nexus. Presented to National Association of Drug Abuse Problems, New York, March, 1982.

Commission on Marihuana and Drug Abuse, *Marihuana: A Signal of Misunderstanding*. Washington: Government Printing Office, 1972.

Davis, F., and Munoz, L. Heads and freaks. *Journal of Health and Social Behavior*, 1968, 9, 156–164.

Domestic Council Drug Abuse Task Force, *White Paper on Drug Abuse: A Report to the President*. Washington: Government Printing Office, 1975.

Drug Abuse Council, *Marihuana Survey, State of Oregon*. Washington: The Council, 1978.

Eddy, N. B., et al., Drug dependence: its significance and characteristics. *Bulletin of the World Health Organization*, 1965, 32, 721–745.

Edwards, A. S. A theoretical and clinical study of so-called normality. *Journal of Abnormal and Social Psychology*, 1934, 28, 366–376.

Epstein, E. J. *Agency of Fear: Opiates and Political Power in America*. New York: Putnam, 1977.

Gordon, B. *I'm Dancing as Fast as I Can*. New York: Bantam, 1980.

Gorer, G. *The American People: A Study in National Character*. New York: W. W. Norton, 1964.

Gusfield, J. R. *Symbolic Crusade: Status Politics and the American Temperance Movement*. Urbana: University of Illinois Press, 1963.

Helmer, J. *Drugs and Minority Oppression*. New York: Seabury, 1975.

Henslin, J. M., and Light, D. W., Jr. *Social Problems*. New York: McGraw Hill, 1983.

Hughes, R. H., and Brewin, R. *The Tranquilizing of America*. New York: Harcourt Brace Jovanovich, 1979.

Johnston, L. D., Bachman, J. G., and O'Malley, P. M. *Monitoring the Future*. Ann Arbor: Institute for Social Research, 1984.

Karmen, A. The drug abuse-crime syndrome: A radical critique, in C. Winick (Ed.) *Sociological Aspects of Drug Dependence*. Cleveland: CRC Press, 1974, 309–319.

Kinsey, A. C., et al. *Sexual Behavior in the Human Male*. Philadelphia: W. B. Saunders, 1948, 660.

Lemert, E. *Human Deviance, Social Problems, and Social Control*. Englewood Cliffs: Prentice Hall, 1967.

Lettieri, D., et al. *Theories of Drug Abuse*. Rockville: National Institute on Drug Abuse, 1980.

Liaison Panel on Psychoactive Drug Use/Misuse, Report to the President's Commission on Mental Health. In L. Brill and C. Winick (Eds.) *Yearbook of Substance Use and Abuse*. Vol. II. New York: Human Sciences Press, 1980, 37–78.

Lindesmith, A. R. *Opiate Addiction*. Bloomington: Principia Press, 1947.

Miller, J. D., et al. *National Survey on Drug Abuse: Main Finding*. Rockville: National Institute on Drug Abuse, 1983.

O'Malley, P. M., Johnston, L. D., and Bachman, J. G. Cocaine use among American adolescents and young adults, in N. J. Kozel and E. H. Adams (Eds.) *Cocaine Use in America*. Rockville: National Institute on Drug Abuse, 1985, 50–75.

Radosevich, M. J., et al. The sociology of adolescent drug and drinking behavior: A review of the state of the field. *Deviant Behavior*, 1980, 1, 145–169.

Ray, O. *Drugs, Society, and Human Behavior*. St. Louis: C. V. Mosby, 1978, 430–431.

Regush, N. M. *The Drug Addiction Business*. New York: Dial, 1971.

Rushing, W. A. (Ed.) *Deviant Behavior and Social Process*. Chicago: Rand McNally, 1969.

Schur, E. M. *Crimes Without Victims*. Englewood Cliffs: Prentice Hall, 1965.

Secretary of Health and Human Services. *Drug Abuse and Drug Abuse Research*. Washington: U.S. Department of Health and Human Services, 1984.

Study finds more unwed couples living together. *The New York Times*, September 16, 1985, All.

Suchman, E. A. The "hang loose" ethic and the spirit of drug use. *Journal of Health and Social Behavior*, 1968, 9, 146–155.

Wegrocki, H. J. A critique of cultural and statistical concepts of abnormality. *Journal of Abnormal and Social Psychology*. 1939, 34, 166–178.

Weil, A. T. *The Natural Mind*. Boston: Houghton Mifflin, 1972.

Winick, C. How high the moon: Jazz and drugs. *Antioch Review*, 1961, 21, 53–68.

Winick, C. The taste of music: alcohol, drugs, and jazz. *Jazz Monthly*, 1962, 9, 8–13(a).

Winick, C. Maturing out of narcotic addiction. *U.N. Bulletin on Narcotics*, 1962, 14, 1–11(b).

Winick, C. The life cycle of the addict and of addiction. *U.N. Bulletin on Narcotics*, 1964, 16, 22–32.

Winick, C. Mass communications and drug dependence. In C. Winick (Ed.) *Sociological Aspects of Drug Dependence*. Cleveland: CRC Press, 1974, 77–102 (a).

Winick, C. A sociological theory of the genesis of drug dependence, in C. Winick (Ed.) *Sociological Aspects of Drug Dependence*. Cleveland: CRC Press, 1974, 3–14 (b).

Winick, C. A labor approach to alcohol and other substance abuse, in L. Brill and C. Winick (Eds.) *Yearbook of Substance Use and Abuse*, Vol. III. New York: Human Sciences Press, 1985, 115–137.

Zinberg, N. E. *Drug, Set and Setting: Theory and Practice of Intoxicant Use*. New Haven: Yale University Press, 1984.

Who Are the Drug Users?

Franklin C. Shontz
James V. Spotts

ABSTRACT. A major void in psychological research is a more precise understanding of who are the drug users. This void has occurred because psychological research has failed to distinguish between the behavior of drug abuse and the psychological characteristics of drug abusers. Although such an understanding will not in itself reduce the incidence of illicit drug use, knowing who the drug users are is crucial to furthering an understanding of some of the factors that contribute to drug-taking behavior. This paper reviews why this void exists, and provides an illustration of how the *Case Study Method* can serve as a means of filling this void. Specifically, the case study method is presented as a scientifically acceptable research procedure that provides information obtained from studying individual human behavior. The case study method is outlined and examples of the kind of information this approach yields are presented.

The title of this article poses an important question, but finding the answer to it will not in itself reduce the incidence of illicit drug use. Knowing who the drug users are is certainly essential to understanding some of the factors that currently make drug abuse a matter of serious social concern. But very little can be said on the basis of research carried out so far that is of much help in describing drug users systematically.

SOURCES OF CONFUSION

Throughout years of research, two sources of confusion have clouded this issue. The first is so obvious that it easily escapes attention. It is that investigators, and those who make and imple-

---

The authors are with the Department of Psychology, University of Kansas, Lawrence, KS 66045.

ment social policies, have not clearly distinguished between the strictly behavioral problem of how to reduce illicit drug *use* and the personological problem of how to describe drug *users* as human beings. Much more time and effort has been expended trying to accomplish the former than trying to understand the latter. Probably that is because society is primarily concerned about reducing illicit drug use. Research and theoretical contributions that seem to promise direct means of reducing the overall level of illicit drug consumption are more appealing than approaches that seem at first glance only to provide deeper insight into the fundamental problems of the human condition. Social planners may perceive these as having little to offer in the way of increasing the power or efficiency of social control mechanisms.

Even investigators who have undertaken the task of searching for psychological correlates or determinants of illicit drug use have often missed the point. They have accepted as their criterion the goal of predicting and controlling drug consumption, per se. Therefore, they have become accustomed to promoting and evaluating their work, and of expecting others to evaluate its worth, mainly in terms of its probable practical consequences. To accomplish their purposes, investigators have adopted the standards and methods of conventional research methodology. By limiting research to correlating scores on tests of psychological traits with measures of level and type of drug use, they have achieved a high degree of operationalism. However, they have lost out on two counts. Little progress has been made toward solving the problem of drug abuse, and investigators seem to have lost sight of, and interest in, the persons whom their qualified variables presumably describe.

The second source of confusion in current attempts to learn who drug users are, is more subtle. Yet, if one really wants to know about drug users, it is both more fundamental and more troublesome than the first. It is fundamental because it is comprehensive and basic enough to account for the limitations of much research that has been carried out on the topic of drug abuse. For example, it accounts for our general failure to learn anything of fundamental importance about drug users, as people, despite expenditures of large amounts of money and years of conscientious research effort.

It is troublesome because, even if the confusion it engenders were cleared up, hope for a simple or single solution to the social problem of drug use would not necessarily increase. The primary benefit to be achieved by removing this source of confusion would be to bring to research on drug abuse (and perhaps to research on certain other socially relevant problems as well) a greater degree of integrity and awareness of its own possibilities and limitations than has been apparent in the past.

Basically, this second source of confusion is a generally accepted chain of assumptive principles, some of which are probably false. In an admittedly oversimplified way, these principles are that once we know who the drug users are, we can find out why they use drugs. That will tell us what causes drug abuse, and once that cause is known, the goal of elimination of drug use can be achieved.

Countless investigators and clinicians have apparently believed this and have convinced granting agencies that, while the goal of controlling drug use may not be just around the next corner, at least the map that each is carrying shows correctly where it is and how to get there. Such practices are likely to lead to confusion because it can justifiably be argued that the various maps which investigators have created on the basis of different theories and methodologies do not all describe the same territory. The paths which different approaches present do not lead to the same, or even to recognizably similar, goals.

When all paths go in different directions, and none take either society or science where it wants to go, sound criteria for either social or scientific evaluation of research plans and outcomes break down. In such a situation, reputation, influence and the ability to turn out a good-looking proposal may become as important as scientific merit in directing the course of research, for no one is in a position to say for certain what scientific merit is.

A particularly disturbing product of the operation of this second source of confusion is a common tendency within each discipline which is engaged in the study of drug use to believe that it possesses the only valid means for understanding the problem. At a more abstract level, it may be said that research is being confused with Truth, physics with metaphysics, theory with description. The babble of clinical, political, popular, and scientific literature, that attests to the reality of this confusion, is open for inspection by anyone who cares to take the trouble to examine it.

Thus, one trait theory answers the basic question, "who are the drug users?", by claiming that the users of substance A are extroverts while the users of substance B are introverts. Other trait theories imply that this is not so. They maintain that drug users are sensation seekers, or novelty experiencers, or change seekers, or they are troubled by low self-esteem. Some more clinically minded points of view may assert that all drug users are sociopaths, or have character disorders or borderline personalities. Others may say that drug users are self-medicators, treating themselves for real or imagined illnesses. Naturally, those who prefer physiological views may say that drug users are physically addicted to the drug(s) they abuse. Epidemiology prefers to see the whole issue as a problem in public health. The drug user is someone who has somehow caught an as yet unfamiliar disease. The disease is not yet fully understood, but its incidence can be traced, its causes can be ferreted out, and appropriate social policies can eventually be established that will inoculate the population against it.

A politician may say that the drug user is one kind of person; the economist says something else. Preachers, ministers or rabbis have their own ideas, as do social workers, counselors and educators. Police officers, judges, prosecutors and public defenders see drug users in ways each believes to be correct. Of course, writers and producers of material for the mass media take pride in the objectivity of their reports, prescriptions, and analyses, few of which agree with each other, either.

Individual members of most diciplines and professions are usually willing to admit that their particular points of view are limited, that they do not know all there is to know about drug abuse. Seeing no way to improve the state of knowledge, some may be willing to let these conditions remain as they are indefinitely. Others may feel that, as a result of vigorous competition among various points of view, the one or two ideas that are most nearly correct will eventually come out ahead of the pack. Still others may have faith that, in some mysterious way, all the findings from all the disciplines will ultimately coalesce into a single, unified, and intelligible whole, though no one is able to say just how that may be achieved.

A MATTER OF PERSPECTIVE

This criticism of current practices and assumptions is not intended as an accusation of bad faith on the part of anyone who is involved in supporting or carrying out research on drug abuse or drug abusers. To interpret it as such would only contribute to and increase the confusion that is at issue and only make it worse. Indeed, agencies that grant funds to support research have often been extremely flexible and considerate. They seem to have recognized that no single approach can produce all the answers. As a result, they have often shown a welcome willingness to let scientific explorers try new approaches, and launch new expeditions to follow new maps, at least until swamps, dead ends or hopeless mazes, that investigators inevitably run into, induce the agencies to abandon support for these adventures and to look around for new maps to try.

The primary issue that has not been faced squarely is all the implications of the simple, and, one would think, obvious fact that *drug users are first and foremost persons*. They are not behaviors to be manipulated or controlled, diseases to be cured, wild animals to be caged, scores on survey questionnaires, variables in equations, constructs in theories, mechanisms to be repaired, or ignoramuses to be educated.

At this point, a possible misunderstanding must be apprehended before it does serious damage. To recognize that drug users are persons is not to condone their behavior. Neither is it to say that some aspects of their behavior cannot be described in terms of physiological processes or psychological test scores. Nor is it to say that none of them are sick, ignorant, dangerous, or evil. It is certainly not meant to deny that anything can be done and that society should therefore feel free of its obligations to control undesirable behaviors, or to care for and protect people who cannot care for and protect themselves.

It is merely to say that drug users, like the rest of us, are complex existential processes. Regrettably, it must be admitted that, even to ask for a simpler or "more objective" answer to the question "who are the drug users?" is to ask for something that cannot be given.

EXISTENTIAL PROCESSES

Saying that people, including drug users, are complex existential processes is tantamount to saying that no matter how carefully they are examined, all attempts to describe or analyze them as human beings will be both arbitrary and incomplete. The feature that makes an existence distinctively human is that it can, to a large degree, become self-determining. Therefore, any effort to explain human existence by referring solely to environmental or biological determinants is certain to be incomplete and contain a high proportion error.

Another important feature of human processes is that they can only be understood in terms of direction and movement. This feature, along with their complexity, and their potential for self-determination, self-direction, and change makes human beings endlessly fascinating but not creatures to be dealt with in quite the same way as one deals with static objects or wholly controlled processes in a laboratory.

Anyone who seeks a simple solution to the problem of drug abuse will find it easy to turn away from this conception of human beings. That is partly because scientists and policymakers have already shown that describing, forecasting, and controlling human actions are possible, at least to some degree and under some conditions. Their limited successes make it difficult to appreciate the inescapable law that description, prediction, and control of human beings are effective only to the extent that the essentially human characteristics of people are ignored, bypassed, or ruled out by the manipulation of conditions. The more isolated the trait or variable studied, the more reliably it can be measured. The larger the group that is studied, the more accurate forecasts of the group as a whole tend to be. The more rudimentary and isolated a behavior, the more easily and thoroughly it can be manipulated and controlled.

Drug use in our society is particularly difficult to manage because it is, to such a large extent, a distinctively human activity. Being a human activity means that, while environmental opportunities and social supports play a part, chronic drug use, particularly of a selective sort, is rarely undertaken by a person solely as a reaction to environmental circumstances. Rather, it is strongly self-determined by the user. Furthermore, drug use is not a response to any instinctual biological urges or drives. Human beings have survived, and even thrived, for hundreds of thousands of years without recourse to heroin, cocaine, barbiturates, or amphetamine.

Given equal exposure and opportunity, people who take drugs do so, by and large, because they choose to. People who do not take drugs do not take them because they deliberately choose to avoid them. As with many important decisions in life, many people do not realize the importance or implications of a choice, at the time the choice is made. What is more, once made, the choice often ceases to seem like a choice. Instead, it is sometimes experienced as a coercive force over which the person no longer can exert control. To anyone who becomes a True Believer in anything, the faith may be freely chosen at first, but it eventually begins to make demands of its own. Nonetheless, the responsibility for the choice remains with the person who made it, not with the object of faith and not with the social or environmental circumstances that supported and encouraged the choice.

HOW TO STUDY A COMPLEX EXISTENTIAL PROCESS

The only way the task of studying drug abusers can be approached systematically is by pretending that human beings are to some degree simpler or less human than they obviously are. The pretense is made manifest by creating an artificial definition of persons and then proceeding to study actual people as if that definition were correct. For example, if people are defined as emitters of respondent behavior, then they are studied with behaviorist theories and techniques. If they are defined as chemical states and processes, they are studied differently than they would be if they are defined as psychosocial entities or as mind-body interactions.

Using this strategy, science promulgates hope for prediction and control of human action by demonstrating that a high level of prediction and control can be attained over the comparatively simple processes that are covered by a proposed definition. Obviously, if people are entities that get sick, then drug abuse may well be a sickness, and the best way to understand drug abusers is to study the "disease" called drug abuse. The technique has worked well in the past in the field of public health. It has not only led to the control of certain diseases but has revealed much about human physiology as well.

Two very important implications of this approach must be clearly understood. The first, and most apparent, is that, if drug users are recognized at the outset to be complex, existential processes, this approach can never give a complete or satisfactory answer to the question posed by the title of this article.

The second implication is less obvious, but more important. It is that, as far as research and social policy are concerned, this approach is the only one we have. Currently, there is no single scientific way to study human beings in all their complexity as existential processes. Nor is there likely to be in the near or distant future. It is necessary to accept the idea that, while progressively increasing knowledge is attainable, the distinctively human aspects of human behavior will never be completely controlled and may never even be fully understood. The only other course would be to undertake programs of social management, similar to those one finds in totalitarian countries, where social controls are deliberately designed to make people into creatures that are less than human. Let us hope that this alternative is out of the question.

The groundwork would be laid for making considerable progress in this area if we accomplished no more than to accept the idea that there are limits to the extent of our possible understanding, prediction and control of human behavior. That would relieve a good deal of the pressure that both scientists and government officials may feel to search for a "final solution" to the drug problem. It would free theoreticians to examine not only the possibilities but also to admit the limitations of their ideas. It would even reduce the need to try to compel people to become what various definitions of them say they should be.

To a large extent, the current answer to the question, "who are the drug users?", is simply that they are whatever we say they are. Furthermore, the more heavily a single preconception of them is touted, the more likely they are to become just what that preconception requires.

A CONTINUUM OF METHODS

Scientific investigators are human beings, and one potentiality of the self-determining process which we call the human being is that of making the most out of what is available. To that end, the following proposal suggests some methodological ideas that would permit the development of a broad scientific program which would maximize the value of research and minimize the extent to which time and resources are spent in the pursuit of illusory goals.

The basic methodological principle, upon which this proposal is based, is familiar to all who have had extensive experience with research on human beings. It is that control over people is gained only to the extent that the investigator is willing to sacrifice complexity, that is to minimize people's choice or self-determination, thereby requiring people to act in ways that are not distinctively human. The converse of this principle is that understanding of people, as complex existential processes, is gained only by giving up the desire to manipulate control or predict their actions with a high degree of precision.

To the philosophically minded, the principle may sound like (though it is not) a restatement of the outworn way of thinking that presumes a polarity of nomothetic (law-seeking) and idiographic (purely descriptive) research. The principle proposed here does not postulate a dichotomy but asserts that there exists a whole spectrum of methodological possibilities that can be drawn upon. At one extreme of this spectrum are narrow-band laboratory studies that confine behavior possibilities and conceptions of the person to the blink of an eyelid or the pressing of a lever. At the other extreme are broad-band clinically relevant case studies that exert little or no control over behavior and are open to virtually all possibilities for understanding. This first principle implies that a comprehensive program of research must deliberately plan for the systematic inclusion and, if at all possible, integration of the full broad range of methodological possibilities.

Stated negatively, the *second* principle behind this proposal is that, when studying human beings, all attempts to achieve either perfect understanding or control must be abandoned at the outset. Stated positively, and more hopefully, this principle asserts that all attempts to achieve limited understanding or control have something to offer and must be taken seriously, provided that every such attempt includes a statement that identifies the outer boundary of its applicability.

The knee-jerk response to this principle may well be to say, "but we already do that." This may be followed by the presentation of a long list of research projects of all kinds that have been generously supported in the past. In the time-honored spirit of Dan Rowan and Dick Martin, we reply "Bullfeathers!"

The variety that is found in current research was not deliberately developed in a systematic fashion. It is not the product of a planned and comprehensive program of scientific research. It was merely accumulated over the years because of unguided changes in fads and fashions, the interests and concerns of some policymakers, and the best perceptions of members of review and advisory committees. Like Topsy, but less successfully, it was not born, it just grew.

A PROPOSAL

A well designed, systematic and comprehensive program of research would not limit itself to narrow purposes but would cover all the possibilities. Its product would not be a prescription for social control, a verified theory of drug abuse, or a disorganized hodge-podge of unintegratable research reports. Ideally, it would result in the construction of a well organized encyclopedia (or, perhaps a library) of information, describing research from a carefully preselected and comprehensive set of projects. These would incorporate the entire spectrum of methodological possibilities. Like all good encyclopedias or libraries, this one would be regularly updated and periodically revised.

The contents of such a compendium of knowledge would be organized along a methodological spectrum, rather than alphabetically, or by subject matter. At one end of this spectrum, it would contain reports of research of the most rigidly controlled, specific and reductionistic sort. At the very beginning of the collection these could be, for example, studies of the physical and chemical properties of substances of interest. Next would come studies of the molecular actions of these substances on specific types of organic tissues, from cells to organ units to organ assemblies. Then would appear findings from research on the effects of the substances on simpler organisms, and then on relatively simple behaviors (pecking, lever pressing, etc.). Next would come reports of results from epidemiological, sociological, and social psychological research on specific actions, characteristics or traits of human beings, studied in groups. These would grade off into anthropological or ethnographic studies of persons in relation to their cultures or environments. Finally, there would be reports of carefully designed and systematically conducted holistic, personological examinations of individuals who use substances for various purposes and in varying amounts or ways.

The organization of reports within each of the subsections of such an encyclopedia or library would probably differ, depending upon the theoretical and methodological demands of research at each level.

Given freedom from the pressures to provide financial aid only for applied research, granting agencies could pay more attention to the systematic accumulation of knowledge, recognizing that the "payoff" of many projects may be as much as five or ten years in the future. Special attention should be paid to encourage research that examines the interface of each level of the methodological spectrum with adjacent levels. Most importantly, care could be taken to see that adequate quantities of high quality research are included at all levels, to insure completeness of coverage.

Given such an encyclopedia or library, an investigator who is interested in physiological research carried out in laboratories would know exactly where to locate information of interest. Similarly, an interested investigator who accepts the idea that drug users can be viewed as individual human beings with distinctively human properties, would know immediately to turn to the person-oriented sector of the spectrum to find summaries, descriptions and reports that are most relevant to his or her needs. Needless to say, however, the current state of affairs is such that this curious investigator would find little there to repay the effort.

One reason that little would be found is that, by and large, current research practices have not been built upon the proposition that methodology is a spectrum but on the proposition that there is only one "true" method in science, and that it is the one adopted at the most reductionistic extreme of control and analysis. All research is judged against this standard; it is the ultimate criterion by which relative scientific merit is measured. Studies of persons, as such, are therefore regarded as being less scientific than studies of groups, variables, factor structures, rates, organs or molecules.

An implication of the proposal made here is that there is not just one but many methodologies in science. Each is related to the one before it and the one that follows it on the spectrum, but each has its own standards of adequacy and scientific merit.

The beginning of this paper suggested that research on persons, as such, has been neglected, in part, because it seems not to hold immediate promise for telling society how to reduce illicit drug use. The point now being made is more fundamental. It is that holistic research on persons has also been neglected because it has seemed less than scientific. In fact, research on persons has been advocated and carried on for years, though not very extensively in the field of drug abuse. Such research makes no effort to manipulate or control variables or behavior, but stresses the careful selection of individuals for examination and both extensive and intensive assessment of all relevant aspects of their functioning. Only one major attempt has been made to carry out this type of research on drug users and the balance of this paper is devoted to describing its purposes, methods, and significant features.

REPRESENTATIVE CASE RESEARCH ON DRUG USERS

Beginning in 1974, and continuing for nearly ten years thereafter, six series of nine studies each were carried out by The Greater Kansas City Mental Health Foundation. Encouragement for undertaking this series of studies came initially from Dr. Daniel J. Lettieri who, at that time, was associated with the National Institute on Drug Abuse. Thereafter, data collection and analysis for the entire series of investigations was supported largely by grants from that agency.

Each study within each series consisted of an examination, in great depth and considerable detail, of the psychological background and characteristics of one extensively recruited and carefully selected person. All the persons examined were adult men ranging in age from about 18 to about 45 years. At the time they were studied, none of the men were hospitalized or incarcerated; all were living independent, though not necessarily legal, lives in the community. In five of the six series of investigations, every person chosen for examination was selected because he was personally committed to the heavy use of a particular drug or a class of drugs and had practiced their regular use over long periods of time. To our knowledge, these studies constitute the first systematic, comparative studies of heavy, chronic drug users in the field of substance abuse.

One group of drug users consisted of men with an intense personal commitment to the chronic use of cocaine. Another contained men whose drug of commitment was amphetamine and its congeners. The third group consisted of men committed to the heavy, chronic use of opiates (primarily heroin), while the fourth group was composed of men who were committed to heavy, chronic use of barbiturates or sedative-hypnotics. The fifth group was composed of nonusers, men who had deliberately chosen not to use hard drugs despite opportunities to do so.

Although each person was studied and understood as an individual, the participants in these first five groups were carefully selected to insure that all groups were as comparable as possible. All five groups were matched (by group) with respect to age, sex, IQ, socioeconomic background, and lifestyle. However, it proved impossible to locate nonusers who were comparable to users in all other respects and educational achievement as well; nonusers tended to have more education than all other groups. The sixth group consisted of heavy, chronic users of phencyclidine (PCP). Despite intensive efforts, it proved to be impossible to match PCP users with the other groups. PCP users were found to be a deviant subgroup within the drug user population. As a group, they were younger, came from lower strata of society, and had more limited work and occupational resources than any of the other groups studied.

Except for those in the PCP user group, the men were drawn from all sectors of society. Each group contained a musician or entertainer; a blue collar worker; a thief, burglar or strong-arm robber; an intense, achievement-oriented individual (a YUPPIE); a manager of performers (musicians, actors, etc.); a scion of an exceptionally wealthy family; an entrepreneur; a social misfit; and a two-worlder, one who maintained legal employment to mask another illegal operation. Diversity of lifestyles within groups justified statements about substance abuse across several different contexts.

Each of these persons was examined for twelve to fifteen full days, over a period of from four to five months. Procedures included extensive life history and drug use interviews and a comprehensive battery of dimensional and morphogenic assessment procedures. Data collection for each cohort of nine men took about one and a half years.

Obviously, these studies yielded many more findings that can possibly be summarized in a few pages of a single report. To describe them all would require at least a full volume of rather large size in an encyclopedia of knowledge about drugs and drug use. A summary of one of the groups alone (cocaine users) has already occupied an entire book. For the interested reader, a bibliography of publications that have emerged from this program of research to date is provided at the end of this article.

Two main purposes are being served by this summary of some aspects of the research program. The first is to show that holistic studies of persons can be carried out with the same careful attention to detail, accuracy, and objectivity as are other forms of research. That being true, studies of persons have as much reason to be included in the methodological spectrum as do any other forms of scientific investigation.

The second purpose served by this summary is to show by example that studying persons as persons can yield knowledge and insight that can be obtained in no other way. For example, the first study series made it quite clear that the effects of a drug taken at high doses need not be a simple quantitative extension of its effects at low doses. Similarly, one person's reasons for taking high doses of a substance on a long-term basis are likely to be qualitatively different from another person's reasons for taking the substance at lower doses or episodically.

DRUG USE HISTORIES

In all the persons studied, the length of time during which they had used drugs of all kinds was greater than the length of time during which they had limited their consumption to their particular substance of choice. Nearly all had begun using drugs by conforming to the pattern that seems typical in late twentieth century urban American communities. Initial usage was in early adolescence and typically consisted of smoking tobacco and drinking alcohol in a variety of forms. Consumption of marijuana and hallucinogenic substances followed, but particular usage patterns and the order of usage of different drugs were determined more by the accessibility and popularity of various substances than by personal preference or choice.

For most of the persons studied in these series of investigations, middle and later adolescence, or even young adulthood, became a period of experimentation and learning. During this period, various substances were investigated in various ways. Their pharmacological properties were learned by garnering information from dealers, friends, more experienced users, or neighborhood experts. One person, who was studied in these series, diligently examined the available drug-relevant literature and became known as a local authority on all aspects of drug use, effects, and sequelae.

By and large, however, these people gauged drug effects by direct experience. Not only were specific substances tried, but mixtures, such as the speedball combination of cocaine and heroin, were taken. Drugs were consumed by different techniques. These young men soon learned that the ''rush,'' produced by a substance such as methamphetamine when injected, is quite different from the effects produced by the same substance taken orally. Both personal experience and vicarious learning, by the observation of others, played parts in teaching these persons the risks involved in drug use, such as the danger of addiction or overdose, problems with the law or drug enforcement personnel, and the consequences of the use of poor quality drugs.

If, at this stage of their experience with drugs, the persons studied in these investigations had happened to serve as subjects in research by a naive investigator, they might have easily been identified as *polydrug* users (usually, a pejorative term). Perhaps they were; the identification has a certain logic; but if these persons were polydrug users, it was only in the technical sense that they had tried more than one substance. In reality, these men were psychologically quite different from what are typically referred to as polydrug users. Although they had tried many drugs, the distinguishing feature of their drug use was its emphasis upon the selection of and continued use of particular substances. Each knew the effects of many drugs but had deliberately chosen to use the drug or class of drug that came closest to meeting central psychological needs. It is hardly surprising that such individuals would experiment with use of a variety of drugs, for without experimentation, choice would be impossible, and it is *choice* that distinguishes the men described in this report from other drug user populations.

THE ISSUE IS PERSONAL COMMITMENT

As suggested by the discussions above, the critical psychological distinction that must be drawn is not based merely on whether a person takes more than one substance, either consecutively or simultaneously, nor does it depend greatly upon how the term substance is defined, in order to facilitate counting for research purposes. The critical psychological distinction is between persons who become personally committed to the long-term use of a specific substance (or combinations of substances) and persons who do not. Psychologically speaking, whether the commitment is based on physiological addiction at the outset does not even matter. The issue of commitment itself is primary. The question of what determines it or how it varies with the use of different kinds of substances (if it does) comes afterward. Obviously, commitment is a personal event. It cannot be studied by questionnaire or by counting specific behaviors (especially during the period of experimentation). Only a careful examination of individuals can reveal whether and to what extent it is present.

LIFE THEMES AND VARIATIONS

On a broader scale, an example of knowledge that can be gained only by studying individuals in depth is provided by the concept of the *life theme*. Most clinicians and investigators who study persons closely become aware very quickly that the life of each person they examine is organized around a few basic themes, or organizing principles.

Research that does not penetrate very deeply into the human psyche may readily identify traits, motives, pathologies or behavioral regularities. The literature abounds with tests designed to do just that. But a theme is not a trait, a thing, or a force. Rather, a theme is a pervasive structural framework which makes traits, motives, pathologies, and behaviors understandable. Drug use means one thing in the life of a person whose theme is that of being a knight errant on a quest for the modern day equivalent of the Holy Grail. It means quite another thing in the life of a person whose theme is that of being a stranger, a wanderer, cast by fate into an alien and complex world he does not understand or one who lives out the theme of the self-sufficient warrior who fights life's struggles alone and can depend upon no one but himself. Drug use means something different still for the person who believes he bears the mark of the Beast and is condemned to live out a life which he himself regards as Evil.

In some instances, life themes seem to be almost deliberately chosen. ("At that moment, I decided that my purpose in life was to do whatever was necessary to defeat my Father.") In other instances, they seem to be imposed from outside the Self. Once a life theme has taken over, though, it assumes a destiny of its own. All that deliberate choice may then accomplish is to make one's fate more bearable. Variations on life themes may be invented; tempos may be speeded up or slowed down; the keys or mode in which a theme is played may be changed; dissonance or harmony may be introduced. But, unless radical changes take place, sooner or later the theme plays itself out and the inevitable comes to pass.

Our studies of these men showed not only how the themes of their lives expressed themselves, but how these persons' use of particular drugs fit into the overall pattern of their existences. Space does not permit more than the mere mention of two published articles that deal with this issue in detail and that could *only* have been derived from intensive studies of individuals. These are the articles on the phenomenology of the ego states induced by two contrasting substances, cocaine and barbiturates (Spotts & Shontz, 1984a, 1984b).

THEORETICAL INTEGRATION

Examinations of life themes in individuals stimulated the development and application of still more integrative ideas about the origins and meanings of drug use. In the course of nearly ten years of research we found that men in the groups we studied differed systematically with respect to (1) early family backgrounds and family dynamics, (2) patterns of adult adjustment, (3) levels of psychological maturity ultimately attained, (4) temporal orientations, (5) types of deficiencies in individuation exhibited as adults, (6) performance on a wide variety of psychological tests, and (7) gravitation to chronic use of drugs that produced strikingly different effects but served quite specific purposes in the user's psychological adjustment. We found that while the concept of life themes was useful, it was not sufficiently broad to encompass all these differences. What was needed was a still more inclusive theoretical framework.

The theory which emerged from our work asserts that the predisposition to commitment to heavy, chronic use of a specific drug or class of drugs originates early in life. It also asserts that these predispositions develop from failure, delays, blockages or only partial successes in meeting the challenges and overcoming the crises of normal individuation. It further states that persons who become committed to heavy, chronic use of specific substance(s) do so because the drug(s) induce(s) a distinctive *ego state* which either allows temporary escape from currently experienced problems or creates the illusion that these problems have been solved by pharmacological means.

Using concepts derived in part from theories proposed by others, this theory has been expanded to include ideas about the overall structure and the process of individual psychological life. The ideas that evolved are not limited in their applicability to drug users, but apply to all human beings, particularly in Western cultures.

FUNDAMENTAL POSTULATES

Our research has led us to conclude that there is an aspect of human existence that quickly becomes apparent when one studies individuals, but that is almost always overlooked in studies of groups. It is the potential for *numinous* experience. Roughly, the word numinous means spiritual. Among drug users, numinous factors are most obvious when drugs are used to produce some form of transcendent experience or are incorporated into quasi-religious rituals. However, numinous factors operate overtly or covertly in everyone's life. They give human existence a mythic quality and lie behind both the search for meaning and the occasional feeling one has of being driven or possessed by life-shaping forces over which personal control is not possible.

Therefore, a fundamental postulate of this theory is that there exists within each individual a counterpart of the Ego, which is called the Self. As the Ego perceptually and motorically relates to external reality, the Self intuitively and creatively relates to the realities of inner life. The *person* is both the battleground upon which Ego and Self struggle for supremacy and the integrated structure within which the two may function harmoniously, at least from time to time.

The Ego must develop through encounters with the outer world. Similarly, the Self must develop through encounters with the world of dreams, myth, and revelation. The fates of the Ego and Self are intertwined. Both must grow and develop if normal psychological individuation is to occur. Consequently, successful personal growth runs a spiraling course that carries the person who is individuating on a generally ascending path, back and forth between these two realities.

Figure l summarizes the basic postulates of this theory. The right side of the diagram represents the outer world, or environment, to which the Ego relates. The left side represents the inner world, or psyche, which is the province of the Self. Being the integrate of these, the *person* is represented at the top of the figure by a bracket that encompasses both Ego and Self.

Two opposing forces or tendencies are represented to the left of the spiral. One, which represents the tendency toward transcendence, is shown as being relatively weak during early life and relatively strong in the later years. The other, which represents chthonic or regressive forces, is shown as being relatively strong during early life and relatively weak later on. These are general tendencies only, because at any point in life when transcendent forces are weakened or blocked, chtonic forces can become dominant, producing a state of stagnation, depression or despair.

The spiral of individuation identifies four major *crises* of personal development, and, as the figure shows, each appears to be

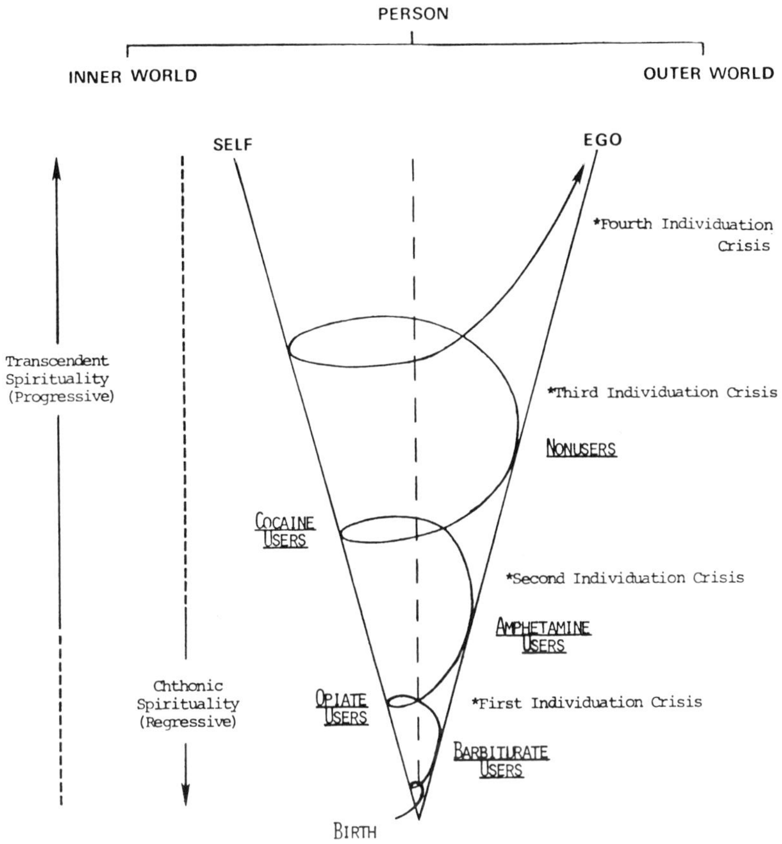

FIGURE 1: The spiral of individuation as related to the core problems of heavy, chronic drug abusers.

Figure 1

associated with the *core* problems of persons who in later life became personally committed to the long-term use of specific drugs or classes of drugs. The theory postulates that in order to individuate the person must undergo these crises, in each of which earlier patterns are radically altered or transformed to permit the emergence of new patterns of attitudes, thoughts, and values that are more appropriate to contemporaneous circumstances. Successful management of each crisis involves a complete cycle of Ego encounter with the external world, return to the inner world of Self, and finally reintegration and movement in the direction of transcendence, as a preparation for the next crisis. Lack of complete success during any crisis does not stop the growth process but does leave psychic wounds that handicap the individual's efforts to resolve succeeding crises in individuation.

The product of successful resolution of the First Individuation Crisis is the establishment of a self-sustaining (though not yet self-reflective) consciousness of separate personal identity. Figure 1 indicates that the core problem of the barbiturate/sedative hypnotic users occurred on the Ego side of this crisis. Never having a separate identity for their own Egos, they were extremely vulnerable to the dark, chthonic forces of the psyche and repeatedly engaged in self-defeating, self-damaging, and even Ego-destructive behaviors. These men seemed repeatedly to tempt Fate to destroy them, and in life history interviews reported an alarming incidence of fights, brawls, accidents, car wrecks, and serious drug overdoses. They described these life threatening events in such a casual fashion that they seemed to care little whether they lived or died. Under stress, they turned to heavy, chronic use of drugs that obliterated the Ego and carried them, ultimately, to a consciousless state of Oblivion.

Opiate users came to grief on the Self side of the First Individuation Crisis. These men had failed to develop an intact, self-reflective Ego or personal identity that is independent of the maternal figure. As adults, these men avoided intense emotionality, did not seem to feel at home in the world and were unable to cope consistently with work, marriage, family, or other adult activities. They showed little interest in adult sexuality even before addiction and preferred to withdraw from the problems of life than attempt to conquer them. Like the barbiturate users, these men found the external world to be too stressful, too complicated, and too demanding. Unlike the barbiturate users, though, these men elected to use substances that pharmacologically would return them to the inner world. Their wish was to restore a primitive paradisical state of peace, contentment, and serenity (metaphorically expressed in religious paintings of the babe asleep at the maternal breast). They turned to use of opiates to find the respite, succorance, and support they needed to tolerate the problems of adult life.

During the Second Individuation Crisis in adolescence, the Ego seeks to free itself completely from close, and often suffocating, dependencies upon the maternal figure. Similar in some ways to the

Oedipal situation described by Freud, this crisis is made especially difficult by the ties of early sexual attractions between mother and child. Typically, it is the father (or, more accurately, the Father Imago) that encourages the breaking free of the child's Ego and its movement into the period of Apprenticeship or preparation for the freedom, autonomy, and responsibilities of adulthood. This process is demonstrated in male initiation rites of so-called "primitive" cultures throughout the world. The product of successful completion of the Second Individuation Crisis is the emergence of an autonomous Ego that is self-reflective, aware of and capable of being responsible for its own actions, capable also of feeling guilt and appreciating the needs and reactions of others.

Amphetamine users had experienced failure in the Ego side of this crisis. They were typically unreflective, action-oriented men who denied their own psychic life, projected their fears onto the environment, and fought them there. They were also locked into a perpetual struggle with the mythic Terrible Mother of Adolescence and the ever-present threat she poses of weakness and impotence. Their psychologically emasculated fathers provided inadequate models of emancipation. The devious and manipulative mothers of these men played out complex schemes of guile and deceit to keep their men under control. These men were drawn to women and seemed fascinated by them. Yet fear permeated all relationships with them. By and large, they conceived women as representative of the Mother of Childhood who, like the sorceress Circe, has the power to convert strong men into domestic swine. Consequently, they viewed women as creatures to be conquered, overcome, used, subjugated, and even punished. Amphetamine users turned to an energizing drug to maintain a high energy level and hypermasculine lifestyle, ward off depression and despair, reinforce strivings for domination, and support the need to constantly disprove their fears of inadequacy.

Cocaine users experienced their core conflict on the Self side of the crisis. These men were proud, ambitious, and competitive individuals, stubborn and willful men who were ready and willing to fight or outwit others to achieve their goals. They were also isolated loners who attempted to deny normal human frailties and avoid dependencies of any kind. Although cocaine users were sexually active, they dominated women and showed little interest in developing mutual relationships with them. These men had broken free from the maternal figure and had achieved independent self-reflective Egos. They had completed the Second Individuation crisis, but were severely scarred by this experience and had never acquired the complete independence of Ego from Self that they seemed to feel was essential. As a result they remained fascinated by the promise of fulfillment but unable to take the next step needed to reach it. For them, the experience produced by cocaine represented, in fact it symbolized, the type of inner ecstasy that most people would expect to receive only during the most profoundly moving type of religious experiences. Cocaine users found the drug-induced experience to be so fully absorbing that they were never able to move beyond it to the next stage of transformation.

Normally, the Third Individuation Crisis occurs when the child accepts and is initiated into the world of conventional adult society. A crisis occurs because, from this point on, the Ego must be fully responsible not only for itself and its own advancement but for continuing the survival of the society within which the person lives. This stage was reached and in some cases surpassed by the nonusers of drugs. The nonusers were aggressive, competent, and self-confident individuals. Each had an heroic dream or a sense of purpose or destiny in his life. These men, unlike the drug users, typically accepted the values of the larger society and saw themselves as having a place in it. Determined to harness their energies and direct their own lives, these men refused to use drugs because they felt that drugs would deprive them of the ability to control their own destinies.

The Fourth Individuation Crisis, if it occurs, it a highly transcendent process that is little understood and rarely studied. The crisis starts when, after achieving conventional success, the Ego begins to question, even to reject, traditional values. The crisis begins with what is commonly referred to as the ''midlife crisis,'' reaches its peak of conflict in the development of a vision of a new and better world that may border on, if not actually become, a delusion of grandeur. The crisis is resolved when a transformation occurs so that balance is restored and the Self functions in equivalence with the Ego. The person is then completely integrated, having given up unrealistic plans of conquest on the Ego side, and grandiose dreams of glory on the side of the Self. Ultimately, the Self gains its opportunity to participate fully in directing ongoing thoughts, feelings, values, and behavior toward personal and social ends that are both transcendent and achievable. As far as we know, none of the men we studied (and very few others, either) had reached this stage of individuation.

SUMMARY AND CONCLUSIONS

The first part of this paper criticized approaches that are currently being taken to attempt to understand people who use and abuse drugs. They were criticized for failing to distinguish between the behavior of drug abuse and the psychological characteristics of drug abusers, for being disorganized, and for aspiring to achieve unrealistic and unattainable objectives. Next, an alternative was proposed in which drug abuse research is organized around the concept of a *spectrum of methodologies*, ranging from the most limited, reductionistic, and impersonal to the most comprehensive, holistic, constructivistic and personal. It was noted that this alternative requires abandoning the expectation that research will or can, produce simple and fully-effective solutions to the problem of drug abuse. The alternative also requires abandoning the outdated notion that science is limited to only one type of method. The product of this proposed approach would be an encyclopedia or library of knowledge that systematically covers all aspects of drug abuse and drug abuser characteristics. To demonstrate that scientifically acceptable research may be carried out at the level of the study of individual human beings, a comprehensive program of personological research that uses the Representative Case Method was described. Its methods were outlined, and a few of its unique contributions were summarized.

REFERENCES

Shontz, F. C. (1976). Single organism designs. In P. M. Bentler & D. J. Lettieri (Eds.), *Data analysis strategies and designs for substance abuse*. (NIDA Research Issue Monograph No. 13, pp. 25–44). Rockville, MD: National Institute on Drug Abuse.

Shontz, F. C. (1978). Single organism research and the representative case method. In D. J. Lettieri (Ed.), *Drugs and suicide: When other coping strategies fail* (pp. 25–44). Beverly Hills, CA: Sage Publications.

Shontz, F. C. (1982). Retrospective family histories of chronic drug abusers. In N. Stinnett, J. DeFrain, K. King, H. Lingren, G. Rowe, S. Van Sundt, and R. Williams (Eds.), *Family strengths. Positive support systems* (Vol. 4) (pp. 497–510). Lincoln, NE: University of Nebraska Press.

Spotts, C. A. (1984). *Personality characteristics and drug experiences of heavy, chronic*

drug users as measured by the Q-sort technique. Unpublished doctoral dissertation, University of Missouri at Kansas City.
Spotts, J. V., & Shontz, F. C. (1976). *The lifestyles of nine American cocaine users: Trips to the land of cockaigne*. (NIDA research Issues Monograph No. 16. DHEW Publication No. (Adm), 76-392). Washington, D.C.: U.S. Government Printing Office.
Spotts, J. V., & Shontz, F. C. (1980a). *Cocaine users: A representative case approach*. New York: Free Press.
Spotts, J. V., & Shontz, F. C. (1980b). A life theme theory of chronic drug abuse. In D. J. Lettieri, M. Sayers, and H. W. Petrson (Eds.), *Theories of drug abuse: Selected contemporary perspectives*. (NIDA Research Monograph No. 30, DHHS Publication No. (ADM) 80-967). Washington, D.C.: U.S. Government Printing Office.
Spotts, J. V., & Shontz, F. C. (1981). Research findings on cocaine use. In G. Volger (Ed.), *Rapture and reality: Drug use in cross-cultural perspectives*, (Vol. II) (pp. 792–795). Cologne: Rauten Strauch-Joest Museum fur Volkerkernde.
Spotts, J. V., & Shontz, F. C. (1982). Ego development, dragon fights, and chronic drug abusers. *International Journal of the Addictions*, *17*(6), 945–976.
Spotts, J. V., & Shontz, F. C. (1983). Psychopathology and chronic drug use: A methodological paradigm. *International Journal of the Addictions*, *18*(5), 633–680.
Spotts, J. V., & Shontz, F. C. (1984a). Drug induced ego states: I. Cocaine: Phenomenology and implications. *International Journal of the Addictions*, *19*(2), 119–151.
Spotts, J. V., & Shontz, F. C. (1984b). The phenomenological structure of drug induced ego state: II. Barbiturates and sedative-hypnotics: Phenomenology and implications. *International Journal of the Addictions*, *19*(3), 295–326.
Spotts, J. V., & Shontz, F. C. (1984c). Drugs and personality: Extraversion-introversion. *Journal of Clinical Psychology*, *40*, 624–628.
Spotts, J. V., & Shontz, F. C. (1984d). Correlates of sensation seeking in heavy, chronic drug users. *Perceptual Motor Skills*, *58*, 427–435.
Spotts, J. V., & Shontz, F. C. (1985). A theory of adolescent substance abuse. *Advances in Alcohol and Substance Abuse*, *4*, 117–138.
Spotts, J. V., & Shontz, F. C. (in press-a). A new perspective on intervention with heavy chronic drug users. *International Journal of the Addictions*.
Spotts, J. V., & Shontz, F. C. Drugs and personality: Dependence of findings on method. (Submitted for publication).
Spotts, J. V., & Shontz, F. C. Drug abuse treatment as an individuation process. In S. Einstein (Ed.), *From theory to practice: The planned treatment of drug abusers*. (Submitted for publication).
Spotts, J. V., & Spotts, C. A. (1980). *Use and abuse of amphetamine and its substitutes*. (NIDA Research Issues Monograph No. 25, DHEW). Washington, D.C.: U.S. Government Printing Office, 1980.

Women: Alcohol and Other Drugs

Edith S. Lisansky Gomberg, Ph.D.

INTRODUCTION

The use and abuse of chemical substances has intermittently been an issue of concern in Western societies. Attitudes toward different drugs have varied over time: when tobacco was introduced in Europe in the 16th century, it evoked strong opposition from the authorities who tried to prohibit its use. When coffee was introduced in the next century, its use was also disapproved. The use of tobacco and coffee became widespread and attempts to prohibit or control the usage gradually diminished.

Although both sexes drank, smoke, and used other drugs, social concerns have traditionally focused on the effects of drugs on male behavior and functioning, and scientific research has had the same foci. Occasional voices may have spoken out about the impairment of women's mothering (e.g., during the Gin Epidemic) but women have been viewed as using drug substances medicinally and social concerns were minimal.

In American history, concern about various drug substances has focused on different ethnic and racial groups. Substance abuse has been linked to newly arrived immigrant groups, to aborigines, Orientals and Blacks. The urban working class saloon, frequented by industrial workers, primarily foreign-born men, came under attack (Kingsdale, 1980). Chinese immigrants were perceived as a threat because of opium use. It was widely believed that cocaine was frequently used by Southern Blacks, and this was not called into question until publication of a report in 1914 of Black admissions to mental hospitals in Georgia (Musto, 1973). In 1901, the United

---

Edith S. Lisansky Gomberg is Professor, School of Social Work, The University of Michigan, Ann Arbor, MI 48109-1285.

States Senate adopted a resolution forbidding the sale of opium and alcohol, " . . . to aboriginal tribes and uncivilized races . . . (including) Indians, Alaskans, the inhabitants of Hawaii, railroad workers, and immigrants at ports of entry" (Sinclair, 1962). There are, to this day, widely held, stereotypical views about the linkage between illegal drugs and different racial and ethnic groups.

Interestingly enough, although there is no evidence of expressed concern about *women and drugs*, anti-drug writings in the 19th and early 20th century make occasional reference to the danger of various drugs present to "youth." Contemporary concern about adolescent drug use has a history a century old: "temperance education" goes back a century. But even the Women's Christian Temperance Union, which was genuinely concerned with many women's issues, concentrated its efforts on male drunkenness and the effects of male alcoholism on the family. Perhaps ignoring women's use of drugs and alcohol was related to the middle class image of women as models of virtue, gentility and self-control.

The purpose of this paper is to provide a review of some of the historical and contemporary events related to problems of women and drugs. It is intended to raise issues that need study and to contribute to a heightened consciousness about women, medication and drugs, still in need of being addressed. The conclusion of this article will be a presentation of research issues and questions arising from the review of the problem of women and substance use and abuse.

WOMEN AND HISTORY [1]

Although the United States had founding mothers as well as founding fathers, it is only recently with the rise of a militant feminist movement, that historians have begun to explore the contribution of the founding mothers. The suffragist movement, and to a lesser extent, the temperance movement, have had some attention, but the contributions to American history of working-class women and women of different races and ethnic backgrounds have had less attention.

[1]It is not ethnocentricity, but limited space that confines this discussion to the history of women in the United States. There is some work on cross-cultural examination of women's roles (Barry, Bacon, & Child, 1957; Rosaldo & Lamphere, 1974).

During the Colonial period, women devoted most of their energies to housekeeping and child care, lived for the most part on farms, and produced large families. As with the European settlers, Native American tribes drew a division between the domestic labors of women and the more public life of men. Black women in slavery were much more likely than White women to engage in outdoor labor; they were sometimes house servants, sometimes field hands, and sometimes both. Most marriages ended with the death of a spouse; divorce was rare although marital disruption did occur with the act of desertion.

Although we now tend to idealize the 19th century pioneer woman, it is probably true that most women simply accompanied their men who had made the decision to move, although some women did move westward on their own. The pioneer wives often dealt with intense loneliness and isolation, and this has been described by several American novelists (e.g., O. E. Rolvaag). In the early waves of immigrants that entered the United States and moved west, women were usually in the minority. Only in moves toward urbanization, which offered some work opportunities to single women and widows, were numbers from both sexes approximately equal. Again, emigrating to large cities required drastic change and adjustment in the lifestyles of women.

The historical roots of women's occupational segregation are described in Boulding's (1976) work on familial constraints on women's work roles, where she described the traditional occupational role as "breeder-feeder-producer." The emergence of capitalism and the patriarchal organization of work assignment may be illustrated by the example of cigar making. Originally a home industry, the early cigar factories employed women who were soon replaced by male immigrants, who in turn were replaced by immigrant Bohemian women working at home. The role of factory management and the role of the union were significant in changing this, once again, to a male occupation (Hartman, 1976).

One historical work suggests that between 1790 and 1840, the American population drank heavily, and this was apparently true of all regions, races, classes, and both sexes (Rorabaugh, 1979). A belief in the nutritious value of alcoholic beverages and a rising abundance of grain created a large supply of cheap whiskey and a large supply of customers. (It was, in Rorabaugh's description, an American equivalent to the British Gin Epidemic which began in 1701.) The per capita consumption of alcoholic beverages declined when a new national grain market appeared (Rorabaugh, 1979), but there may well have been other reasons for the decline, e.g., the growth of a temperance movement.

The middle of the 19th century brought an expanding development of the Industrial Revolution and a simultaneous development of a strong, woman-headed temperance movement. Women demonstrated a talent for organization in a number of 19th century movements: abolitionist groups, anti-child labor and prison reform groups, Utopian communities, and temperance societies. The phenomenal rise and success of the Women's Christian Temperance Union has been linked to several different historical phenomena: moral reform bent on improving the lot and behavior of the working class, a change in family structure, and the new view of alcohol as a dangerous drug. Although the Women's Christian Temperance Union was concerned with *drunkenness*, there was little said about intoxication or problem drinking by women. Presumably only fallen women and prostitutes used alcoholic beverages intemperately and they were beyond redemption, i.e., fallen angels. The temperance movement was concerned with the male drunkard and the effects of his intemperance on the family. Under the leadership of Frances Willard (1879–1898), the WCTU worked for woman suffrage, prison reform, facilities for neglected children, and federal aid to education. The eventual success of the movement, culminating in the Prohibition Amendment to the U.S. Constitution in 1919, demonstrated that well-organized women's movements can and do wield power effectively. Prohibition also demonstrated that prohibiting a substance that many people want to use is not an effective way to stop the use of that substance.

The 20th Century

From the viewpoint of women's history, this century may be divided into two periods, pre-World War II and post-World War II. The first decade of the 20th century was the end of the Victorian period, and the first two decades were the peak and the tapering off of the European migrations to the United States. The 1920s, presumably the decade of the "flapper," seemed to be a period of increasing freedoms for women, e.g., smoking in public became more socially acceptable. The large majority of poor, working class and lower-middle class women were largely unaffected by "the flapper age." The either-or choice, job *or* marriage, continued for all women. In 1920, only 12 percent of all professional women in the United States were married. In 1924, 75 percent of women earning a Ph.D. degree were single (Berkin, 1979). One has only to look at the plays (Moss Hart's "Lady in the Dark") or movies of the 1920s and 1930s, to see the theme of the achieving woman who gives up her career and finds fulfillment in marriage. Some of the films of Spencer Tracy and Katherine Hepburn stand out as exceptions, however, suggesting the possibility that women could express their work talent and have a loving relationship at the same time.

The Depression of the 1930s re-evoked the argument that women worked for "pin money," and in 26 states bills were introduced to prohibit married women from working outside the home. This came about although women's jobs were largely domestic, menial, and not competitive with men's work.

World War II created an unprecedented demand for women's labor. A decade earlier it had been her patriotic duty to leave jobs for men to do; now it was her patriotic duty to work at such jobs. From 1940 to 1945, the proportion of women in the work force rose from 25 percent to 36 percent. Furthermore, among the six million women working outside the home for the first time, many were engaged in skilled jobs in heavy industry (e.g., "Rosie the Riveter"). When the war ended, dismissal and pressure to resign reduced the percentage of women in the workplace, but not without resistance. Not only were societal demands shifting, the workplace itself was changing and labor needs pulled women toward "pink collar" work, i.e., toward clerical and service jobs. During the 1950s, the pressure on women to leave the workplace and return to full-time housewifery and mothering was reflected in much of the social sciences: a number of social problems such as juvenile delinquency and emotional disorders of young people was attributed to mothers in the workplace. Nonetheless, there was resistance against being displaced and an interesting contradiction: in the 1950s, white middle-class women were marrying at an earlier age than their grandmothers had done, but at the same time there were more women working outside the home than ever before. These were not often women with young children at home; the movement of these young women toward the workplace began a decade later.

It is not necessary to reiterate the statistics about the ever-mounting proportion of the American labor force that is female. The increasing presence of women in the workplace, the astronomical rise in divorce rates, the increase in single, female-headed households and one-parent families, have been well documented. Moynihan's description of the female-headed households among Blacks created a storm of controversy (Rainwater & Yancey, 1967), but it is as appropriate today as it was when written. The sexual revolution has created freedoms, but men as well as women are "liberated," and one interpretation of male liberation is abdication of the traditional male role of economic responsibility for children of divorce.

Almost parallel with these developments has been a sharp increase in societal concern over women's alcohol and drug usage. The concern comes in part from the feminist movement, which emphasizes the papering over and neglect of women's problems in this area. Feminists have also called attention to issues related to women's use of prescribed and psychoactive drugs. But, societal concern is primarily with abusive use of alcohol and illicit drugs.

WHY THE CURRENT CONCERN ABOUT WOMEN AND DRUG ABUSE?

As noted above, pressure was exerted on women in the workplace when World War II ended to return to their traditional homemaker roles. Although women had demonstrated their competence in wartime industry the old issue of *lesser ability* arose again. Review of research on male/female comparisons on a variety of performance tasks led to the conclusion, as early as 1946, that the differences were exaggerated:

> Scientific evidence available . . . fails to indicate differences attributable to such membership that would justify casting men and women in different social roles. (Seward, 1946, p. 245)

Although men and women tend to differ in patterns of abilities such as girls manifesting greater verbal ability, and boys excelling in visual-spatial and mathematical ability, the overlap is enormous, and the conclusion that women are less trainable, less competent, less talented than men is unwarranted. The sexes do differ in patterns of ability, but differences in achievement appear to be much more related to socialization, drive to achieve, and access to the opportunity structure.

In the same post-World War II period, the social science/psychoanalytical literature about the consequences of inadequate mothering burgeoned. Mothers working outside the home, it was argued, are inadequate nurturers and the resultant deprivation contributes importantly to juvenile delinquency, behavior disorders, neuroses, alcoholism and schizophrenia, among other unhappy conditions. As summarized by Hays (1964):

> Women have been admitted into industry and white-collar work in large numbers. . . . Nevertheless, the controversy still goes on as to whether the working mother can be a successful housewife, whether her children suffer from this situation, whether her abilities are inferior to those of men, in short men are simply not happy about her economic freedom. (p. 270)

The first heralds of the new feminism were Friedan's book, *The Feminine Mystique* (1963), and Rossi's (1964) essay on equality between the sexes. Rossi's essay is a critique of the psychoanalytically-influenced social scientists who promoted the image of the "healthy" woman adult as one *exclusively* devoted to marriage and parenthood. So a new feminism was born, generated partly by the rebellious challenge to conventional ways and norms and by the civil rights movement of the 1960s.

In the twenty years which have passed, progress has been made in women's economic status. Women are more visibly present in some professions. More women are in the workplace (albeit in low-level and dead-end jobs). Affirmative Action programs exist. A woman has also been nominated by the Democratic Party for Vice President in the 1984 election campaign. Progress may be slow, but it is visible. Parallel with this progress has been a mounting public, governmental, and media concern about female substance abuse. It is true that insofar as alcoholic beverages are concerned, the percentage of American women who drink (in any quantity) has risen from midcentury to the 1970s (Gomberg, 1974). But, that percentage has levelled off and a survey conducted in 1981 found no evidence of any major increase in women's drinking over the time period 1970 to 1981 (Wilsnack, Wilsnack, & Klassen, 1984). It is difficult to judge whether there has been an increase in women's use of narcotics or other illegal drugs because the number of such drug abusers which appear in the literature are, admittedly, estimates. Use is made of medically-prescribed mood-modifying drugs by both sexes; but from the inception of their use women have been the larger users. Public and governmental concern does not seem to extend to women's use of prescribed psychoactive drugs, e.g., minor tranquilizers. Concern has focused on women's drinking and women's use of illicit drugs.

The current concern about women's substance abuse seems to be linked to several different phenomena. *First*, it should be pointed out that concern has grown almost proportionately with female progress in the workplace, and this suggests that economic competition may be one important factor promoting concern. *Second*, a growth industry of substance abuse treatment facilities, professionals and paraprofessionals has developed, and while much of the concern about female substance abuse is genuine, it is also good for business. *Third*, the federal government has created two federal agencies to deal with problems related to alcohol and drugs, and again, mixed with genuine concern is the necessity for a bureaucracy to justify its existence and Congressional committees to justify their expenditures. And finally, there has been a long history of association between female intoxication and immorality, and a longstanding belief that the woman alcoholic is "sexually promiscuous." When alcohol is involved in a rape, there is considerable difference in social attitudes depending on whether the rapist or the victim has been drinking: it appears to be more forgivable when the rapist has been drinking (loss of control!) and less forgivable when the victim has been drinking (Marolla & Scully, 1979).

It appears that the present high degree of concern about women's drinking and use of illicit drugs may also be linked to societal hostility and to backlash, relating to rapid change and shifts in sex roles. Such a linkage is hypothetical and difficult to document. Marris (1974), however, has described "the conservative impulse"—the sense of loss which accompanies swift and marked social change and the deep need to maintain continuity in goals and relationships. It is a tenable hypothesis that the feminist movement and the visible and rapid changes in sex roles have produced a sense of loss in many men and women. Coexisting with change in sex roles are shifts that have occurred in family structure, in sexual permissiveness, and in adolescent freedoms—all sources of societal concern. Changes in female sex roles may indeed have produced a backlash in which the challenge to the traditional female role is seen as producing a host of familial and social problems, including substance abuse among women.

Deeply-rooted anxieties and ambivalence about women's behavior is not new, but the increased competition with men for economic benefits and for power appears to have intensified this anxiety and ambivalence. The presence in the workplace of married women with children still creates controversy, yet the statistics show an increasing proportion of women returning to or entering the workplace while their children are still very young. The disturbance this evokes appears to manifest itself in a counterattack: breaking out of the traditional role of housewife/wife/mother produces not only delinquency and emotional disorder in children and adolescents, it produces the drinking and drug abuse which are destructive to the fetus in utero. There is less attention and handwringing about the misery of the woman substance abuser than there is about "addicted babies" and fetal alcohol effects. A disproportionate number of research dollars have gone into fetal effects, leaving other research areas relatively neglected. Granted the toxic effect of heavy drinking and narcotic, sedative and stimulant abuse on the fetus, it still needs to be pointed out that negative effects of prescribed medication (thalidomide?) have come in for less concern and attention. And, if it is the health of infants which touches deeply into public concern, the relatively high rates of infant mortality among nonwhite groups in the United States should cause a great outcry, but they do not.

CURRENT STATUS: WOMEN'S USE OF SUBSTANCES

Since patterns of usage vary with different substances which may be more or less socially acceptable, use of substances in five different categories will be summarized: (a) prescribed medication in general, (b) prescribed psychoactive drugs, (c) over-the-counter (OTC) medication, (d) the "social" drugs: tobacco and alcohol, and (e) illegal or "street" drugs. Comparisons of men's and women's use of substances indicate that women consume more prescribed and psychoactive medications than do men, and that women consume less of the "social" drugs and the "street" drugs. There are some age variations which relate to different stages of the life span and to cohort/generational differences, and there are social class and regional differences as well. What follows is a brief review of some of these issues.

Prescribed Medication

Several reports have dealt with the relationship between the physician and the female patient (e.g., Corea, 1977). A recent study compared male physician response to five medical complaints made by men and women patients in their forties: back pain, headache, dizziness, chest pain, and fatigue. With an equal number of physician visits, "men received more extensive workups than women in all five of the complaints" (Armitage et al., 1979, p. 2187). The authors suggest that the physicians may be responding to "current stereotypes" in which the male is "typically stoic" and the female "typically hypochondriacal."

Are prescriptions more readily written for the female patient? Is it that women make more physician/clinic/hospital/office visits, and therefore, are more likely to receive a prescription? Are women patients more likely to want, and communicate that wanting, of medication to the physician? While the reasons are difficult to establish, it is clear that women use more prescription drugs than men, and this is true in spite of the fact that women have more adverse drug reactions even when controlling for dose and number of drugs prescribed (Simpson et al., 1978; Hamilton & Parry, 1983).

Verbrugge's (1982) report, that women use more legal drugs of all types than men do, is primarily linked to morbidity and age. "Personal characteristics" also contribute to the sex difference in the amount of drug use. Such "personal characteristics" of the women include: being slightly older than the men in the study, having less active social roles, experiencing more disruptive events and more morbidity, considering their health to be worse, feeling more helpless about life, and, being unable to ignore symptoms as easily.

Prescribed Psychoactive Drugs

One of the best documented facts in the study of women and drug use is the relatively large number of mood-modifying, psychoactive drugs prescribed for women. The national survey conducted by Parry et al. (1973), indicated that 13 percent of the men and 29 percent of the women had reported using "psychotherapeutic" prescription drugs during the past year. Many studies have reported responses of women and men in the United States and Canada, but the greater female use of psychoactive drugs is by no means confined to these two countries. Cooperstock (1971) indicated higher prevalence of use by women in the United Kingdom as well as in the United States and Canada. Balter, Levine, and Manheimer (1974) surveyed the use of "anti-anxiety/sedative" drugs in nine European countries and reported the percentage of women who had used psychoactive drugs during the past year as approximately twice the percentage of men.

Even with this impressive consistency of results, there are questions. Cooperstock (1975) raised the question of under-reporting in survey response as well as the question of "hidden" psychotropic drugs, i.e., mixed drug preparations containing a psychotropic agent as well as a substance intended for some somatic condition. Clearly, however, women receive more prescriptions for mood-modifying drugs. There is no decisive answer whether this is due to more physician visits by women patients, to physicians' stereotypes and attitudes toward their male and female patients, or to women patients' greater desire and demand for medication. Perhaps all of these combine to produce the male-female ratio of use of psychoactive drugs.

Over-the-Counter (OTC) Drugs

The use of patent medicines is very difficult to document and researchers may have to rely on more drug company records than user information. Prescription drugs are usually a matter of record and prescription statistics have been used in research. Prescriptions involve writing by the physician and producing the medication by the pharmacist. OTC drugs, however, are sold in drug stores, supermarkets, general stores, department stores, etc. From the information which is available, there may be more use by women than by men, particularly in the age group 15 to 44 (Bush & Rabin, 1976). Young men appear to purchase a relatively large amount of stimulant OTC drugs. Among people over 60, there appears to be small gender difference in purchase and use.

Some reports suggest that although there are no overall sex differences in use of mood-modifying OTC drugs (Burt, Glynn, & Sowder, 1979), some variations may occur. Men, for example, are more likely to purchase drugs like Nodoz, whereas women are more likely to be using prescription stimulant drugs (amphetamines). It will probably be evident that the male-female ratio will vary with particular classes of OTC drugs: antacids, analgesics, antihistamines, vitamins, etc. If the incidence of colds or respiratory illnesses in general is examined up to age 3, boys have more; from that age on, women always have more colds or respiratory illnesses (Monto & Ullman, 1974). One of the most popular self-medications is NyQuil, which commands 25 percent of the market (Ray, 1983). This OTC remedy, which contains 25 percent alcohol, may represent an updated equivalent of the 19th century tonics for women.

The "Social" Drugs: Tobacco and Alcohol

1. Tobacco

Men and women have both shared in the ritual use, and later the secular use, of tobacco in almost all cultures, especially in Western societies. In industrialized nations, women are fast approaching men in the rate of initiation and prevalence of tobacco use. This trend began in the 1920s in the United States (Nuehring & Markle, 1974).

Among adolescents in general, initiation into smoking during preteen or teenage years is chiefly social in origin. More smoking occurs among lower income and low-achieving students, and among those who are more likely to drink alcoholic beverages. From the mid-1960s to the mid-1970s little change occurred in the pattern of boys' initiation into and maintenance of smoking. The overall change in adolescent regular smoking, which went from 4 percent in 1968 to 32 percent in 1974, was "almost entirely due to increased smoking among teenage girls" (Gritz, 1980). In addition, there has been a sharp increment in the proportion of *heavy* smokers among females age 13 to 35. Among adults, there has been a gradual decline during the 1960s and 1970s in the percentage of males who smoke, but there has been very little change among women (Schuman, 1978). The following is of some demographic interest: women's smoking is more prevalent among higher income groups, while men show the opposite trend. Among young women 18 to 35 years of age, housewives smoke more heavily than employed women. While there is still a higher percentage of smokers among men, the gender differences are small: for the 12 to 17 year olds, 12 percent of the girls and 13 percent of the boys use cigarettes; for the 18 to 25 year old age group, the percentages are 40 percent for women and 45 percent for men, and for adults 26 years of age and older, 33 percent of the women and 41 percent of the men smoke cigarettes (Fishburne, Abelson, & Cisin, 1979).

2. Alcohol

One must distinguish between drinking per se and problems created by drinking alcoholic beverages. For temperance believers, *any* drinking is harmful and sinful: "total abstinence is the only safe way to avoid the evils which alcohol engenders" (Fundamental Facts Concerning Beverage Alcohol, 1956, p. 8).

Surveys of American drinking practices (Cahalan, Cisin, & Crossley, 1969; Clark & Midanik, 1982) indicate that about two-thirds of Americans 18 years of age and older drink and that most of them consume alcoholic beverages in small and moderate quantities which do not cause problems for themselves or others. Epidemiologists and other social scientists have distinguished such drinkers from "heavy drinkers" and from "problem drinkers."

Now, when we look at women's use of alcohol, are we talking about infrequent and moderate drinking or about alcoholism? It is true that the percentage of American women who drink has risen from midcentury up to the 1970s when the percentage leveled off (Leland, 1982). Evidence about a rising prevalence of heavy, alcoholic drinking, however, is more equivocal.

It is not always clear whether the handwringing and the viewing with alarm has to do with women's drinking per se or with heavy drinking, intoxication and alcoholism. Certainly problem drinking is just that: a problem which is devastating for both women and men and their families. But are we speaking of excessive use or any use at all? Most ascetic religious groups frown upon drinking by either sex. But other, more permissive groups, seem to be reasonably accepting of women's drinking *in limited quantity*. The Talmud states this quite clearly:

> One cup of wine is good for a woman;
> Two are degrading;
> Three induce her to act like an immoral woman;
> And four cause her to lose all self-respect and sense
> of shame. (The Talmud [The Study of the Mishna]) [2]

[2]I am indebted to Mark Keller, Editor Emeritus of the *Journal of Studies on Alcohol*, for the Talmudic reference.

When we examine prevalence of problem drinking and alcoholism among women, the numbers are estimates. It is true that more women have entered rehabilitation facilities and Alcoholics Anonymous during the last decade than they did before that, but readiness to seek treatment does not necessarily mean an increase in prevalence. Some surveys have reported a relatively high percentage of heavy/frequent drinkers among women in the workplace (Johnson, 1982), but the relationship between employment outside the home, part-time work, unemployment, housewife status, and drinking, is not really clear. What is clear is the ominous note sounded in Fillmore's (1984) statement that,

> heavy-frequent drinking is more common in the younger age groups as compared to older cohorts measured at the same age . . . the youngest cohort, who in 1979 were ages 21–29, seem to show a much higher rate of heavy-frequent drinking than past cohorts measured at the same age, particularly among the employed. (pp. 29, 31)

Coupled with these epidemiological findings is the observation of an increasing proportion of young women who appear in substance abuse treatment facilities. It appears that in those facilities to which women come for help, the mean age is no longer in the forties—as it was a generation ago.

Is it possible that the proportion of American women who drink (as compared with the proportion who are abstinent) remains constant while the proportion who drink problematically rises in the young adult age group? What are the consequences? Will these young women go on to become middle-aged alcoholics? Will treatment head off the progression of alcoholism, begun relatively early in life? Will the youngsters who are now 10 to 19 years of age maintain the same "much higher rate of heavy-frequent drinking" as the current group of women who are now in their twenties, or will they show even higher or perhaps lower rates of heavy-frequent drinking? These questions certainly suggest that we turn our attention and effort toward *prevention*.

There have been many reviews of the literature on female alcoholism (e.g., Lindbeck, 1972; Gomberg, 1974; Shaw, 1980; Ferrence, 1980).

Illegal or "Street" Drugs

Prior to the passage of the Harrison Act in 1914, there were apparently more, perhaps twice as many, women who used narcotics heavily (Martin & Martin, 1980). The typical "opiate addict" in the 19th century and up to 1914 was

> a 30 to 50 year old white woman who functioned well. . . . She bought opium or morphine legally at the local store, used it orally, and caused few, if any, social problems. She may have ordered her "family remedy" through the mail from Sears Roebuck—two ounces of laudanum for 18 cents. (Ray, 1983, p. 334)

At the present time it is estimated, admittedly a guess, that women comprise about 20 to 25 percent of the addict population, numbering more than 100,000 women. The percentage of persons over 18 using heroin is calculated at 1.8 percent of men and 0.6 percent of women (Burt, Glynn, & Sowder, 1979). In 1969, the gender ratio of males to females for those entering treatment for narcotics addiction was four to one; by 1980, it had become three to one. The image of the typical heroin addict as a young adult Black male is apparently changing: in 1969, admissions to treatment facilities consisted of 55 percent Blacks and 30 percent Whites; by 1980, this had become 30 percent Blacks and 58 percent Whites. The age of addicts, at least those in treatment facilities, has also shifted downward: in 1969, adolescents under 18 constituted 6 percent of admissions to treatment programs, young adults 18 to 25 constituted 37 percent of admissions. In 1980, the proportion of adolescents admitted to treatment programs had gone up to 13 percent and the proportion of young adults down to 30 percent.

The male-female ratios of "lifetime users" (ever used) of cocaine, hallucinogens, inhalants, marijuana, and hashish show a larger percentage of boys than girls among adolescents 12 to 17 years of age. Among adults, males also show a higher prevalence of use. Although "lifetime use" of these drugs is higher for men, sex differences with respect to *current* usage are small (except for marijuana). Thus, it appears that a higher proportion of women who try these drugs continue to use them after they are first tried. Male users, however, use larger quantities than female users. In summary, more men have tried illicit drugs and take larger doses of drugs, but many claim that, " . . . The sexes are involved with them in equal percentages at present" (Fidell, 1982).

The current situation relating to the use of *cocaine* has developed so rapidly, there is little reliable information about the usage by men or women. There is no question about the rapid escalation of its use. During the 1970s, the "ever used" incidence appeared to have tripled in all age groups. By 1980, estimates were that 28 percent of young adults between 18 and 25 had used cocaine, a third of them within the previous month. Cocaine overdose deaths have multiplied within recent years: between 1980 and 1983, San Francisco reported a 300 percent increase in cocaine overdose (Smith, 1984). Several patterns of use have been identified: experimental use, recreational use, situational use, intensified drug use and compulsive drug use (Siegel, 1977). High school seniors who reported ever having experimented with cocaine increased from 9 percent in 1975 to 17 percent in 1981, and Ray (1983) believes that use by adolescents and young adults will continue to increase. Available information indicates that cocaine, like other illegal drugs, has more male users than female users. Concern has been expressed by health authorities about increasing use of cocaine by women.

The male-female ratio of *"designer drug" use* is not known; such drugs having appeared so recently as drugs of abuse that statistics about prevalence have not been obtained. It is to be expected that more males will be experimenting with these new drugs as they appear, although some women, probably heroin addicts, will be experimenting with them as well.

WHAT IS DRUG ABUSE?

Drug abuse is usually defined in terms of heavy alcohol consumption and/or use of illicit drugs—and the consequences of such use. Drug abuse is deviant behavior and, as Gusfield (1967) points out:

> Deviant designations have histories; the public definition of behavior as deviant is itself changeable. It is open to reversals of political power, twists of public opinion, and the development of social movements and moral crusades. What is attacked as criminal today may be seen as sick next year and fought over as possibly legitimate by the next generation. (p. 187)

A 19th century woman might have ordered laudanum from a Sears & Roebuck catalogue, but a 1985 woman probably has a supply of minor tranquilizers, sedatives, and stimulants ordered by prescription from a pharmacist. Marijuana has gone from ''Reefer Madness,'' cause of depravation and insanity, to very widespread use and acceptance; it may be legalized before the century is out. Alcoholics have gone from being viewed as weak-willed and immoral sinners to being accepted as people with a ''disease.'' In Los Angeles, it is positively stylish, if you are well-to-do and abusing alcohol or cocaine, to go to the Betty Ford Center for rehabilitation (Corkery, 1985).

A differentiation needs to be made between the *therapeutic* and the *recreational* uses of drugs. (There is also a religious use made of drugs like peyote by the Native American Church, but few Indians or non-Indians use alcohol, cocaine, tranquilizers, etc., for religious purposes.) This differentiation between the therapeutic and recreational use has not changed over time: when women used opiate-laced tonics as medication for a variety of disorders, there was no outcry. Nor is there a current outcry about relatively heavy female use of psychoactive drugs. Feminists may protest that women are overmedicated, but it is really not considered a social problem. Nor is it viewed as a medical problem; women are at higher risk for adverse drug effects, e.g., tardive dyskinesia (Simpson et al., 1978) and negative drug interaction effects, but that has little apparent effect on the number of prescriptions written.

In terms of defining women problem drug users, consider Woman ''A'', for example, who is a regular user of minor tranquilizers and sedatives or who is taking prescribed antidepressant drugs, and Woman ''B'' who smokes two packs of cigarettes a day. By current standards, neither presents drug problems. However, Woman ''C'' who drinks frequently and heavily, and Woman ''D'' who is a user of cocaine or heroin, *are* considered problem users. Women ''C'' and ''D'' are, in fact, considered ''sicker'' and more deviant than their male counterparts (Karpman, 1948; Gomberg, 1974; Rosenfield, 1982).

The fact that women are viewed differently than male drug abusers raises the question whether a substance is being used for medicinal or recreational purposes. Women may be stigmatized for their apparent hedonism but the fact is that women appear to use virtually all drug substances in more or less medicinal ways. Kolb (1938) commented fifty years ago that women used opiates to relieve, " . . . mental and physical distress," whereas men were more likely to use opiates recreationally, i.e., for the pleasure involved. There is, of course, a component of relief-of-distress in men's use of substances just as there is pleasure-seeking in women's use. But our hypothesis remains: *women tend more frequently to use substances in medicinal, therapeutic ways than do men*, and they tend to do this because of patterns of social approval and disapproval. Gender socialization orients women and men toward different patterns of drug use and even toward different substances. Women, generally being more law-abiding than men, gravitate toward more legally acceptable, socially-acceptable substances such as cigarettes, alcohol, and use of prescriptive drugs.

To sum up, women are users of prescription drugs, psychoactive drugs and patent medicines to a greater extent than men, but this is not viewed as drug abuse; it is medication. The heavy use of alcohol and/or illicit drugs is disapproved whether it occurs among women or among men—that *is* drug abuse. And a widely-held view is that such drug abuse, i.e., heavy use of alcohol and/or illicit drugs, is *more* disapproved by society for women than for men (Lisansky, 1957; Gomberg, 1974; Fillmore, 1984).

What follows is a discussion of some of the issues and questions linked to the problem of greater female than male use of medication and psychoactive drugs. Then I will present some of the viewpoints and explanations that have been offered about the problematic use of alcohol and illicit drugs by women. Finally, I will raise a number of research questions dealing with women and drug substances, questions which I believe need to be answered.

WOMEN AND MEDICATION

The Physiological Events in Women's Lives

It is a fact of life that the biological stages of the life span are more clearly marked for women than for men. Men's biosexual lives are also phased, but the phases are not as clearly defined as the menstrual cycle, pregnancy, childbirth and lactation, and menopause. These are not only *biological* events, they are events surrounded by folk beliefs, myths, and attitudes. In many cultures the menstruating woman is perceived as "unclean," and is often isolated during her period or required to cleanse herself ritualistically at its termination. At the end of the last century Havelock Ellis observed that it was still believed that menstruating women would despoil religious rites, sour milk, spoil the wine fermentation, and cause plants to die (Hays, 1964). Research attempts to pin down the relationship between stages of the menstrual cycle and efficiency of performance, moodiness, depression, psychiatric symptoms, and suicide attempts, have produced ambiguous results at best. There have been some interesting attempts to link stages of the menstrual cycle to psychoanalytical dream interpretation, to suicide, and to blood alcohol concentration (Benedek & Rubinstein, 1939; Wetzel & McClure, 1972; Jones & Jones, 1976).

There are several levels on which this linkage between women's physiological cyclical life events and the prescription of medication may be approached. There are women's own perceptions of these events, and there are the perceptions of others, including the perceptions of physicians or other health caretakers. Many women turn to analgesics, diuretics, and tranquilizers at stages of the menstrual cycle. It is women who take "the pill" to avoid contraception and other pills to stimulate fertility. It is women for whom estrogen and similar substances have been prescribed in menopause. Yet reliable information about the effects of various prescribed drugs on hormonal or behavioral responses is minimal (Halbreich et al., 1984). Women themselves share in the social attitudes and mythology about menstruation, and while some women do indeed experience pain and discomfort, menstruation, pregnancy and menopause are, for most women, normal biological events that do not necessarily require psychoactive medication. I have argued that substance use for pleasure, for erotic enhancement, or for "highs" has not been sanctioned for women, but medicine is always permitted. It is difficult to decide whether educational campaigns directed toward lessened use of psychoactive medication for normal physiological cycles should first target the women themselves or the caregivers in order to reduce the misuse of psychoactive substances. Physicians, however, will continue to prescribe tranquilizers as long as women wish to use them. Perhaps increasing economic independence will produce a recognition of the physiological events in women's lives as normal, healthy events for most women, which will not require self-medication or excessive reliance on physician's prescription pads.

The Relative Health Status of Men and Women

Women experience more acute illness, and men have more serious chronic conditions and more injuries during their lifetimes. The data on chronic medical conditions present a mixed picture: women after age 45 have more chronic illness than do men. Men, however, have higher prevalence rate for "killer" conditions, i.e., major causes of death (Verbrugge, 1981).

Gender-defined social roles lead to health risks, including hazards, lifestyle behaviors, and role-linked stresses. Such roles also define health attitudes and the availability of medical/health care. Verbrugge (1982) has included both "real morbidity" and "perceived morbidity" as producing differences in the sexes' use of medication. There are sex differences in exposure to hazards, in lifestyle behaviors, in role-linked stresses, in health attitudes, and in use of the health care systems. Probably the most significant difference lies in *health attitudes*: in general, women seem more concerned about health problems, and their socially-defined role behaviors do not encourage the kind of stoicism (and denial of symptoms) which is part of men's "macho" behavior. Women consistently report worse health status than men do. Women use more outpatient health services, make more visits to a physician per year, are more likely to have a regular source of medical care, and are more likely to seek psychiatric help. The importance of visits to physicians as related to use of prescribed medication has been demonstrated (Bush & Osterweis, 1978). The differences of physicians' attitudes toward medical complaints by men and by women has also been demonstrated (Armitage, Schneiderman, & Bass, 1979).

It would appear that gender differences in "real morbidity," perceived health status, use of physicians' services, and attitudes of physicians all play a role in producing the gender differential in prescription practices. Questions have been raised: since women use health services more, is the difference in prescription medication based primarily on the greater frequency of visits? Cooperstock (1976) has pointed out that:

> recent statistics in Ontario indicate that greater use of physicians' services by women is an inadequate explanation of the higher rate of prescribing psychotropic drugs. (p. 760)

Another question is, do women request drugs more often than do men? Again, data are scarce, but one report does suggest that women patients *sought* and received more drugs than male patients (Winstead et al., 1974).

The issue of relative health status of the two sexes is further complicated by other demographic variables, such as age, education, employment status, and marital status.

Mental Health Issues

It is hardly necessary to reiterate the consistent finding of higher prevalence of depression in women or to review the epidemiology of suicide. Women make more suicide attempts than men, but men are more often suicide completers than are women. There is disagreement as to whether women have higher rates of mental disorder than men. Gove and Tudor (1977) concluded that rates were higher for women, but Dohrenwend and Dohrenwend (1977) have concluded that sex differences in *overall* rates of mental illness are nonexistent. The issues seem to revolve around the question of whether investigators include "personality disorders" or not. Rates are higher for women when they are excluded from mental illness counts.

Although there are many works about gender and mental health issues (e.g., Gomberg & Franks, 1979), it is necessary to distinguish between disordered, diagnosable, symptomatic behaviors on the one hand, and "psychological distress" on the other. *Diagnosable mental disorders* may occur with approximately equal frequency in both sexes, although particular disorders will vary in prevalence by gender. But there is a great deal of evidence that *psychological distress* occurs more frequently among women than among men (Selected Symptoms, 1970). The question is whether the prescription of psychoactive drugs, minor tranquilizers, sedatives, stimulants, antidepressants, etc., is really warranted as medication for psychological distress. The highest risk candidates for depression among women are young poor women with young children at home, unemployed, and often with very little emotional or any other kind of support (Brown & Harris, 1978). Are these problems solved with medication, with tranquilizers? Even if a biological/genetic vulnerability to mild depression is demonstrated, are tranquilizers the solution?

Sex Roles, Health, and Medication

The physiological events in women's lives and their physical, mental, and economic health are all part of a socially-assigned role, i.e., the responsibilities and the rights, privileges and immunities assigned to each of the sexes. In a way, it is ironic to describe housewives and homemakers as living a "traditional role," because women have always worked outside the home, on farms, in factories, or as slave labor, and inside the home as immigrant home industry workers. It is a recent historical development that defines the feminine role as exclusively homemaker. The rise of a large middle class in the affluent, industrialized countries produced that definition.

Insofar as use of substances is concerned, it appears that use of medication and very moderate use of intoxicants by women are acceptable in Western societies. Intoxication, pleasure seeking, and heavier use of substances is not acceptable. If a pregnant woman ingests a prescribed substance which does fetal damage (thalidomide), society reacts with sympathy, but no blame is attached to the woman or the physician. If, however, she uses heroin or drinks heavily during a pregnancy, she has voluntarily chosen this course and therefore carries societal censure. Fetal impairment, whether transient, moderate or severe, is attributable to her lack of control and self-indulgence.

Even single episodes of intoxication may be taboo, counter to assigned female role. In a cross-cultural comparison of sex roles, Child, Barry, and Bacon (1965) commented,

> It seems reasonable to expect that most societies would limit drinking and drunkenness in women more than in men. Under the general prevailing conditions of human life, temporary incapacity of a woman is more threatening than is temporary incapacity of a man. For example, care of a field can be postponed for a day, but care of a child cannot. The general social role of the sexes makes drunkenness more threatening in women than in men. (p. 60)

Certainly for the helpless infant nurturant care may not be postponed. But intoxication threatens many different kinds of behaviors: indeed the care of a crop or a hunt may be postponed, but if it threatens the food supply of a community, it is no small matter.

Another aspect of assigned female role is that of caretaker of the sick and the old, but the relationship between this and female medication use has not been worked out. Szasz (1974) wryly comments on the fantasy of, "male parthenogenesis . . . of the birth of medicine," and adds that, "although the noble priest-physicians of antiquity are no doubt the far-distant ancestors of the modern medical scientist, his next of kin is his mother—the medieval white witch" (p. 62). Whether woman's role in a society is shaman/healer/white witch or caretaker, there would appear to be a link between these roles and women's attitudes and practices surrounding medication (Gomberg, 1982).

How does the nurturer obtain nurturance? How do women satisfy their needs for nurturance? A cross-cultural survey of sex differences in socialization (Barry, Bacon, & Child, 1957) reports that of the 110 cultures studied, in 82 percent of the cultures, socialization for "nurturance" is greater for girls. In no culture was socialization pressure toward "nurturance" found to be greater for boys than for girls. "Responsibility" training in socialization was greater for girls in 61 percent of the cultures studied; for boys, in 11 percent. Current studies indicate that the average working woman spends more time at work and works harder than does the average working man (ISR Newsletter, 1977). For married women in the workplace, there are dual work role responsibilities—in both Marxist and capitalist societies.

It is suggested that one way of obtaining nurturance in a legitimate, socially-acceptable way, is through perceived illness and resulting health care and medication. A socially-permissible way for the woman nurturer to be taken care of is to be sick, to seek health care, to seek and take medication. Perhaps there is a symbolism in the drugs women are prescribed.

WOMEN AND DRUG/ALCOHOL ABUSE

Before discussing some of the explanations of women's substance abuse, it is worth emphasizing the "invisibility" of women's problems. This would appear to contradict the assertion that the last decade has witnessed a mounting concern about women's substance abuse (the concern mixed with blame and attributions to emancipation). Women's problems are invisible in the sense that the focus, concern, and research are almost always on the male; the female counterpart has until recently been ignored. Thus, in 1957 when I published some findings about women (Lisansky, 1958), there were only four research reports about the woman alcoholic and, years later, when Sandmaier titled her book on female alcohol abuse, *The Invisible Alcoholics* (1980), it was still an appropriate adjective. The sex bias in alcoholism research has been pointed out many times and the relatively fewer facilities available to women alcoholics and drug abusers has also been pointed out.

This is not unique to substance abuse. A book about "shopping bag ladies" (Rousseau, 1981) comments about the invisibility of homeless women. A recent review of the literature on alcohol and sexuality (Gomberg, in press) revealed a paucity of research literature about alcoholism and homosexual men, but virtually nothing on the alcoholism of lesbian women. Nor is "invisibility" confined to women with problems. A recent letter from a woman business executive which appeared in *Working Woman* magazine (March, 1985) describes the behavior of a male visitor to the company laboratory: "it was as though I did not exist" (p. 33). Women, as Simone de Beauvoir (1953) and others have pointed out, constitute "the second sex."

There is relatively little research literature on women substance abusers compared to male substance abusers, but speculation and theorizing about why some women abuse drugs and alcohol do exist. Some of these explanations are biological, some psychodynamic, others sociocultural, and probably the most useful of all are those explanations which integrate these viewpoints. The origins of behavior, acceptable and unacceptable, are more complex and multilayered than can be explained by any one discipline.

Biological Explanations

More work has been done on the genetic predisposition toward female alcoholism, perhaps because there are more women with alcohol problems than with narcotics dependence. Two reports about genetics and female alcohol abuse have appeared (Goodwin et al., 1977; Bohman et al., 1981). There is general agreement that for both men and women "there is a hereditary factor in alcoholism" (Holden, 1985). While a hereditary factor has not been specifically elucidated for women narcotics addicts, it is likely, at a time when studies are regularly reporting genetic factors in criminality, smoking, food likes and dislikes, etc., that a genetic factor will also be discovered to explain women's narcotic addiction.

There have also been explanations of alcoholism in terms of nutritional, vitamin or enzymatic deficiencies, or in terms of body build. A study which appeared 30 years ago (Fleetwood, 1955) reported the existence of a "resentment substance" in the blood which diminished in alcoholics when they drank. More recent work on the metabolism of alcohol and biochemical effects is summarized by Roach (1982), Majchrowicz (1982), and Lieber (1982). It would appear that the biochemical response to alcohol and to drug substances may be different among high-risk and low-risk people. This is work in progress.

Psychodynamic or Psychological Explanations

Although *psychoanalysis* offered an explanation of male alcoholism in terms of "early oral fixation," there was no theory to account for femal alcohol/drug problems. As with psychoanalytic theory in general, the reasoning was that if it explained the male, it explained the female. Explanation was rooted in distortion of the early mother-child relationship. If female development is described in terms of passivity and masochism (Shainess, 1984; Caplan, 1985), do these constructs underlie substance abuse? Perhaps Menninger (1938) offered a theoretical construct relevant to female alcoholism in his description of alcoholism as self-destructive behavior. Suicide attempts are frequent among women substance abusers and their low self-evaluation often appears clinically in self-abasing behaviors.

Learning theory and social learning theorists have focused on the role of alcohol as a tension reducer, in minimizing anxiety, fear, and conflicting feelings. Drinking behavior and alcoholic behavior are learned because they are reinforced. In later stages of problem drinking one reward of alcohol lies in postponing the unpleasant effects of withdrawal. Social learning theory also deals with the social environment, i.e., the cultural norms with which a person grows up and the stresses which are experienced. Learning theory is presumably equally applicable to both men and women.

A promising current line of explanation deals with *stress and coping mechanisms*. It is now understood that the term "*stress*" is too broad, and that distinguishing between different kinds and amounts may be useful. One classification is of stress as chronic, acute and "daily hassle" stress, while another is of stress as physical interpersonal, internal, or environmental. We are coming to understand that a stressful *event* by itself explains little; the meaning and significance of stress is in the *response* to the event, the *experience* of stress, i.e., in distress. A useful model of stress and coping has been drawn by Maracek (1978). An event not experienced as stressful does not necessitate coping, but if the event *is* experienced as distress the question then is whether the individual can cope successfully. Those who are poor copers with minimally-effective defenses against stressful experience are at higher risk for the development of psychological disorders, including substance abuse. Ongoing research with women alcoholics in treatment facilities and a group of control women suggests that there are significant differences between the two groups in the experience of stress and in the repertoire of responses for coping with stress (Gomberg, in press).

One category of stresses which has recently had some attention is sexual trauma. Whether men and women are more likely to become drug abusers when there is a history of sexual abuse and whether this is more relevant as an explanation of female alcoholism than of male alcoholism, are questions.

Related to explanations dealing with stress and coping mechanisms are concepts dealing with social supports and social networks. The application of these concepts to explanations of female substance abuse should be productive.

One explanation of substance abuse is the existence of particular *personality traits* manifested by individuals who became substance abusers. This explanation assumes that the traits preexist the substance abuse and indeed are part of the etiology. A review of this literature indicates that the characteristics identified so far are impulsivity, nonconformity, gregariousness, and poor self-concept (Barnes, 1979). Supporting evidence is uneven, but the behaviors involved in impulsivity and poor impulse control as related to the development of drinking problems do seem to have sound data support. Studies of adolescent substance use have noted the relevance of impulsivity (Honzik, 1984), and studies of adolescent substance abuse have stressed the importance of impulsive personality style (Zucker, 1979). Impulsivity and antisocial behavior have been compared among adolescent girls and adolescent boys (Zucker & DeVoe, 1975). One of the few longitudinal studies of women raises the question of impulsivity and impulse control (Jones, 1971). Ongoing research studies of women alcoholics in treatment facilities show an early history of difficulties in impulse control. Compared with nonalcoholic women, the alcoholic women have run away from home more often, dropped out of school earlier, made significantly more suicide attempts, etc. (Gomberg, in press).

As an explanation of female substance abuse problems, *gender role* and problems generated by sexually-assigned role have come in for a good deal of recent attention. Sex role explanations have varied widely: drug abuse among women has been attributed to overidentification with the *traditional* role (''hyperfemininity''), to adoption of a nontraditional ''*emancipated*'' role with its freedoms and responsibilities, to *conflict* over traditional versus nontraditional sex role styles, and to *dual role burdens* usually borne by married women working outside the home who work a regular workday and then come home to domestic responsibilities. Female substance abuse has also been linked to the low level, low status, unstimulating occupations in which a very large percentage of women work.

One direction of sex role explanations has been the equation of stereotypes of women's behavior with characteristics of depression. Whether sex role socialization is linked to women's depression is a question. There is no question about the linkage of depression and substance abuse. Depression runs through the literature on female alcoholism, and depressed mood is apparently characteristic of women narcotics addicts as well. Since mild depression characteristically occurs more often among women than among men, the question is why does depression sometimes lead to greater substance abuse among women? Another question is, why does depression occur more frequently among women?

It should be noted that many behaviors repeatedly reported in the literature of female substance abuse are included in the psychological explanations: feelings of distress and depression, inadequate coping mechanisms, low self-esteem, impulsivity and difficulties related to sex role. It is not always clear whether they are antecedent to or a consequence of substance abuse.

Sociological Explanations

People grow up and mature within a family, a primary group with particular characteristics and particular interactions. This is the family-of-origin, early social environment. *Socialization* is a developmental process in which attitudes, beliefs, and behaviors relating to drug substances, as well as to all other aspects of life, are learned from others. Nor is the process restricted to the family. Early on, the child begins to learn from his/her peers, and pressures to drink or to experiment with drugs often come from peers. Coping mechanisms are also learned during this process of socialization. Although there are similarities, the processes and goals of socialization differ for the two sexes; clearly, this is how sex roles are learned. Socialization theories probably are most closely linked to sex role, stress, coping, and are consistent with social learning theory explanations of substance use and abuse by women.

Sociocultural theories are based on the literature of ethnic and religious group differences in drinking. Demographic (gender, age, education, etc.) and anthropological studies of various subgroups within the United States (Irish, Italians, Jews, Chinese, etc.) have produced consistent results over time. Sociocultural theory goes back to Bales' (1946) exposition of three factors which he believes determine a group or society's use of alcohol and drugs: the level of tension within the group, the norms relating to substance use, and the degree to which the group offers alternatives to deal with stress. This view would link to sex role and social learning theories in a psychosocial, integrated theory seeking to explain substance use and abuse.

Social deviance theory has viewed deviant behavior such as substance abuse as socially-defined behavior, i.e., "conduct which is generally thought to require the attention of social control agencies" (Erikson, 1964). Deviance is not intrinsic to the behavior, but is a property conferred on the behavior by society. Persons who are labeled "delinquent" or "alcoholic" continue to engage in those roles. Since deviance is defined by the social group in any given time and place, it is interesting to note the different directions such labeling may take. When a society defines alcoholism as a "disease," that society has determined that alcoholic persons have an "illness" and are therefore entitled to a "sick" role.

It seems to be true that female deviants are considered less worthy than male deviants, and there is literature on "stigma" which supports that view. Generally, men and women receive more severe societal reactions when the deviant behavior is inconsistent with traditional sex role norms: men, for example, are more likely to be hospitalized for depression, women for substance abuse (Rosenfield, 1982). One form of deviance theory speaks of "blaming the victim," and interprets disordered or deviant behavior as a response to oppressive conditions. Cloward and Piven (1979), for example, explain female deviant behavior as "hidden protests . . . and resistance" (p. 651).

When one considers biological, psychological, and sociological explanations of substance abuse, it is clear that each set of theories has only limited applicability. The most productive course of action is to integrate explanations in a theory which will explain vulnerability to substance abuse problems in terms of a person's biological, psychological, and social history and characteristics (Gomberg & Lisansky, 1984).

RESEARCH QUESTIONS

Having reviewed some of the available information about women's use and abuse of various substances and having stated some of the explanations offered to explain the origins of substance abuse among women, I would recommend priority status for several research questions.

1. Definition and elaboration is needed in the distinction between *medicinal and recreational use of drug substances*. When does a social use of a substance shift to use of the same substance to reduce tension, ease psychic pain, or heighten emotions? Does addiction carry with it the component of medicinal use to diminish the painful withdrawal from the drug? Is the context in which a drug is used critical in determination of whether it is used medicinally or recreationally? Perhaps motivation theories are relevant, but will one set of motivations explain the socially-acceptable use of a substance like alcohol and the deviant, excessive, problematic use of it as well?

2. Since we have a fair amount of evidence that, at particular stages of a pregnancy, heavy drinking or heroin-addictive behavior produce *teratogenic risks*, the research question becomes one of determining the effects of prescribed medications, sedatives, stimulants, psychoactive drugs, and even patent medicines, on fetal development (e.g., Cooper, 1978; Chasnoff et al., 1983). Considering the number of women involved, it is important to know about the effects of mood-modifying drugs and other medications on fetal development. And still considering teratogenic risks, an important research question is: What is the effect of the father's heavy alcohol or drug use on the fetus?

3. Epidemiologists have given us data about *gender differences in*

psychotropic drug use. Further questions include: When men and women show the same symptomatic behaviors, are chemotherapeutic drugs prescribed equally or differently for the two sexes? To what extent are mood-modifying drugs being prescribed for insomnia, anxiety, boredom, loneliness, loss, stress, i.e., for the human condition? Do prescribing practices show gender differences among younger people, young adults, the middle aged and the elderly? Are medical practitioners, who prescribe psychoactive drugs more frequently than other physicians, more likely to hold stereotypical views of male and female character? What is the relationship between development of a new psychoactive drug by a drug company, the advertising, the activity of the "detail persons," and the extent to which physicians write prescriptions for the new drug?

4. *Changes in the workplace*: probably the single most important change in female role has been the increasing presence of women in the workplace. This has had positive effects for women, yet it has also been reported that problem drinking has significantly higher rates among employed married women than among single working women or housewives (Johnson, 1982). Recent work contradicts the latter finding, reporting "no evidence of unusually-heavy drinking among working wives" (Wilsnack, Wilsnack, & Klassen, 1984). It would seem to be a good time to begin clarifying the issues involved in women's working outside the home and women's use of alcohol and drugs. In which occupational classifications is "role overload" most likely to occur? Is substance abuse more likely to appear more frequently in those occupations with least prestige, low wages, little power? Are women in higher prestige managerial positions likely to respond to heightened pressure and drive for achievement with more drinking and/or drug use? What is the relationship between employment, use of medical care resources, and the use of drug substances?

5. *Psychological theory clarification*: although the terms are widely used, there is need for definition and classification of stresses, of coping mechanisms, of social supports. How do these phenomena interact?

6. *Prevention efforts* are called for, particularly for adolescents and young adults. To what extent may we utilize the current trends toward health promotion and the current interest in fitness, diet and exercise to combat drug abuse? Can we design programs that will be effective in lowering the number of cirgarette smokers among young women, as well as moderating their drinking? Can we design

programs targeted to persons at high risk for alcohol and other substance abuse problems?

These questions represent only a few of the many research problems that need to be addressed. The tasks are enormous. Are we up to the challenge?

REFERENCES

Armitage, K. J., Schneiderman, L. J., & Bass, R. A. (1979). Response of physicians to medical complaints in men and women. *Journal of the American Medical Association, 241*, 2186–2187.

Bales, R. F. (1946). Cultural differences in rates of alcoholism. *Quarterly Journal of Studies on Alcohol, 6*, 480–499.

Balter, M. B., Levine, J., & Manheimer, D. I. (1974). Cross-national study of the extent of antianxiety/sedative drug use. *New England Journal of Medicine, 290*, 769–774.

Barnes, G. E. (1979) The alcoholic personality: a reanalysis of the literature. *Journal of Studies on Alcohol, 40*, 571–634.

Barry, H., Bacon, M. K., & Child, I. L. (1957). A cross-cultural survey of some sex differences in socialization. *The Journal of Abnormal and Social Psychology, 55*, 327–332.

Benedek, T. & Rubinstein, B. B. (1939). Ovarian activity and psychodynamic processes. *Psychosomatic Medicine, 1*.

Berkin, C. R., & Norton, M. B. (Eds.). (1979). *Women of America: a history*. Boston: Houghton Mifflin.

Bohman, M., Sigvardsson, S., & Cloninger, C. R. (1981). Maternal inheritance of alcohol abuse: cross-fostering analysis of adopted women. *Archives of General Psychiatry, 38*, 965–969.

Boulding, E. (1976). Familial constraints on women's work roles. In N. Blaxall & B. Regan (Eds.), *Women and the workplace* (pp. 95–117). Chicago: University of Chicago Press.

Brown, G. W. & Harris, T. (1978). *Social origins of depression, a study of psychiatric disorder in women*. New York: The Free Press.

Burt, M. R., Glynn, T. J., & Sowder, B. J. (1979). *Psychosocial characteristics of drug-abusing women*. DHEW Publication No. ADM 80-917. Rockville, MD: National Institute on Drug Abuse.

Bush, P. J., & Osterweis, M. (1978). Pathways to medicine use. *Journal of Health and Social Behavior, 19*, 179–189.

Bush, P. J., & Rabin, D. L. (1976). Who's using nonprescribed medicines? *Medical Care, XIV*, 1014–1023.

Cahalan, D., Cisin, I. H., & Crossley, H. M. (1969). *American drinking practices: a national study of drinking behavior and attitudes*. New Haven: College and University Press.

Caplan, P. J. (1985). *The myth of women's masochism*. New York: Dutton.

Child, I. L., Barry, H., & Bacon, M. K. (1965). Sex differences in a cross-cultural study of drinking. *Quarterly Journal of Studies on Alcohol*, Supplement No. 3, 49–61.

Chasnoff, I. J., Burns, W. J., & Schnoll, S. H. (1984). Perinatal addiction: the effects of maternal narcotic and nonnarcotic substance abuse on the fetus and neonate. *45th Annual Meeting of the Committee on Problems of Drug Dependence. N.I.D.A. Research Monograph No. 49*, 220–226.

Clark, W. B., & Midanik, L. (1982). Alcohol use and alcohol problems among U.S. adults: results of the 1979 national survey. In *Alcohol consumption and related problems*.

NIAAA Alcohol and Health Monograph No. 1. Publication No. ADM 82-1190, Washington, D.C.

Cloward, R. A., & Piven, F. F. (1979). Hidden protest: the channeling of female innovation and resistance. *Signs: Journal of Women in Culture and Society, 4*, 651–669.

Cooper, S. J. (1978). Psychotropic drugs in pregnancy: morphological and psychological adverse effects on offspring. *Journal of Biosocial Science, 10*, 321–334.

Cooperstock, R. (1971). Sex differences in the use of mood-modifying drugs: an explanatory model. *Journal of Health and Social Behavior, 12*, 238–244.

Cooperstock, R. (1975). A critical examination of two studies of psychotropic drug consumption. *Addiction Res. Foundation Substudy 716.*

Cooperstock, R. (1976). Psychotropic drug use among women. *Canadian Medical Association Journal, 115*, 760–763.

Corea, G. (1977). The hidden malpractice: how American medicine treats women as patients and professionals. New York: William Morrow and Co., Inc.

Corkery, P. J. (1985). Addiction a L.A. mode. *The New Republic*, July 8, 1985, 18–21.

De Beauvoir, S. (1953). *The Second Sex*. New York: Knopf.

Dohrenwend, B. P., & Dohrenwend, B. S. (1977). Reply to Gove and Tudor's comment on 'Sex differences in psychiatric disorders'. *American Journal of Sociology, 82*, 1336–1345.

Erikson, K. T. (1964). Notes on the sociology of deviance. In H. S. Becker (Ed.), *Perspectives on Deviance: The other side*. New York: Free Press.

Ferrence, R. G. (1980). Sex differences in the prevalence of problem drinking. In O. J. Kalant (Ed.), *Alcohol and Drug Problems in Women*. (pp. 69–124). New York: Plenum.

Fidell, L. S. (1982). Gender and drug use and abuse. In I. Al-Issa (Ed.), *Gender and psychopathology*. (pp. 221–236). New York: Academic Press.

Fillmore, K. M. (1984). "When angels fall": women's drinking as cultural preoccupation and as reality. In S. C. Wilsnack & L. J. Beckman (Eds.), *Alcohol problems in women* (pp. 7–36). New York: Guilford Press.

Fishburne, P. M., Abelson, H. I., & Cisin, I. (1979). *National survey on drug abuse: main findings, 1979*. Rockville, MD: National Institute on Drug Abuse.

Fleetwood, M. F. (1955). Biochemical experimental investigations of emotions and chronic alcoholism. In O. Diethelm (Ed.), *Etiology of chronic alcoholism* (pp. 43–109). Springfield, IL: Charles C. Thomas.

Friedan, B. (1963). *The feminine mystique*. New York: Norton.

Fundamental facts concerning beverage alcohol. (1956). Columbus, OH: Lewis C. Berger.

Gomberg, E. S. (1974). Women and alcoholism. In V. Franks & V. Burtle (Eds.), *Women in Therapy* (pp. 169–190). New York: Brunner/Mazel.

Gomberg, E. S. L. (1982). Historical and political perspective: women and drug use. *Journal of Social Issues, 38*, 9–24.

Gomberg, E. S. L. (forthcoming). Alcohol, gender and sexual problems: an interface. In W. M. Cox (Ed.), *Treatment and prevention of alcohol problems: a resource manual*. New York: Academic Press.

Gomberg, E. S. L. (in press). Women and alcoholism: psychosocial issues. In *Proceedings of the National Research Conference on Women and Alcohol*, Seattle, Washington, May, 1984.

Gomberg, E. S. & Franks, V. (1979). (Eds.), *Gender and disordered behavior*, New York: Brunner/Mazel.

Gomberg, E. S. L. & Lisansky, J. M. (1984). Antecedents of alcohol problems in women. In S. C. Wilsnack & L. J. Beckman (Eds.), *Alcohol problems in women* (pp. 233–259). New York: The Guilford Press.

Goodwin, D. W., Schulsinger, F., Knop, J., Mednick, S., & Guze, S. B. (1977). Psychopathology in adopted and nonadopted daughters of alcoholics. *Archives of General Psychiatry, 34*, 1005–1009.

Gove, W. R., & Tudor, J. F. (1977). Sex differences in mental illness: a comment on Dohrenwend and Dohrenwend. *American Journal of Sociology, 82*, 1327–1336.

Gritz, E. R. (1980). Problems related to the use of tobacco by women. In O. J. Kalant (Ed.), *Alcohol and Drug Problems in Women* (pp. 487–543). New York: Plenum.

Gusfield, J. R. (1967). Moral passage: the symbolic process in public designations of deviance. *Social Problems, 15*, 175–188.

Halbreich, U., Asnis, G., Goldstein, S., Nathan, R. S., Zander, K. & Herne, J. V. (1984). Sex differences in response to psychopharmacological intervention in humans. *Psychopharmacology Bulletin, 20*, 526–530.

Hamilton, J. A., & Parry, B. (1983). Sex-related differences in clinical drug response: implications for women's health. *Journal of the American Medical Women's Association, 38*, 126–132.

Hartman, H. (1976). Capitalism, patriarchy and job segregation by sex. In N. Blaxall & B. Regan (Eds.), *Women and the workplace*. Chicago: University of Chicago Press.

Hays, H. R. (1964). *The dangerous sex: the myth of feminine evil*. New York: G. P. Putnam's Sons.

Holden, C. (1985). The neglected disease in medical education. *Science, 229*, 23 August, 1985, 741–742.

Honzik, M. P. (1984). Life span development. In M. R. Rosenzweig & L. W. Porter (Eds.), *Annual review of psychology* (35) (pp. 309–331). Palo Alto: Annual Reviews, Inc.

Johnson, P. B. (1982). Sex differences, women's roles and alcohol use: preliminary national data. *Journal of Social Issues, 38*, 93–116.

Jones, M. C. (1971). Personality antecedents and correlates of drinking patterns in women. *Journal of Consulting and Clinical Psychology, 36*, 61–69.

Jones, B. M. & Jones, M. K. (1976). Alcohol effects on women during the menstrual cycle. *Annals of the New York Academy of Sciences, 273*, 576–587.

Karpman, B. (1948). *The alcoholic woman*. Washington, D.C.: Linacre Press.

Leland, J. (1982). Gender, drinking, and alcohol abuse. In I. Al-Issa (Ed.), *Gender and psychopathology*, (pp. 201–236). New York: Academic Press.

Lieber, C. S. (1982). Medical issues; the disease of alcoholism. In E. L. Gomberg, H. R. White, & J. A. Carpenter (Eds.), *Alcohol, science and society revisited* (pp. 233–261). Ann Arbor: University of Michigan Press.

Lindbeck, V. L. (1972). The woman alcoholic: a review of the literature. *The International Journal of the Addictions, 7*, 567–580.

Lisansky, E. S. (1958). The woman alcoholic. *Annals of the American Academy of Political and Social Science, 351*, 73–82.

Majchrowicz, E. (1982). The role of blood in alcohol intoxication and addiction. In E. L. Gomberg, H. R. White, & J. A. Carpenter (Eds.), *Alcohol, science and society revisited* (pp. 171–185). Ann Arbor, MI: University of Michigan Press.

Maracek, J. (1978). Psychological disorders in women: indices of role strain. In I. H. Frieze, J. E. Parsons, P. B. Johnson, D. N. Ruble, & G. L. Zellman (Eds.), *Women and sex roles: a social psychological perspective* (pp. 255–276). New York: W. W. Norton & Co.

Marolla, J. A. & Scully, D. H. (1979). Rape and psychiatric vocabularies of motive. In E. S. Gomberg & V. Franks (Eds.), *Gender and disordered behavior: sex differences in psychopathology* (pp. 301–318). New York: Brunner/Mazel.

Marris, P. (1974). *Loss and change*. New York: Pantheon Books.

Martin, C. A., & Martin, W. R. (1980). Opiate dependence in women. In O. J. Kalant (Ed.), *Alcohol and drug problems in women* (pp. 465–485). New York: Plenum.

Menninger, K. (1938). *Man against himself*. New York: Harcourt, Brace & Co.

Monto, A. S., & Ullman, B. M. (1974). Acute respiratory illness in an American community. *Journal of the American Medical Association, 227*, 164–169.

Musto, D. F. (1973). *The American disease: origins of narcotic control*. New Haven: Yale University Press.

Nuehring, E. & Markle, G. E. (1974). Nicotine and norms: the reemergence of a deviant behavior. *Social Problems, 21*, 513–526.

Parry, H. J., Balter, M. B., Mellinger, G. D., Cisin, I. H., & Manheimer, D. I. (1973). National patterns of psychotherapeutic drug use. *Archives of General Psychiatry, 28*, 769–783.

Rainwater, L., & Yancey, W. L. (1967). *The Moynihan report and the politics of controversy*. Cambridge, MA: The M.I.T. Press.

Ray, O. (1983). *Drugs, society and human behavior*. St. Louis: Mosby.

Roach, M. K. (1982). The biochemical and physiological effects of alcohol. In E. L. Gomberg, H. R. White, & J. A. Carpenter (Eds.), *Alcohol, science and society revisited* (pp. 17–37). Ann Arbor: University of Michigan Press.

Rorabaugh, W. J. (1979). *The alcoholic republic: an American tradition*. New York: Oxford University Press.

Rosaldo, M. Z., & Lamphere, L. (Eds.) (1974). *Women, culture and society*. Stanford, CA: Stanford University Press.

Rosenfield, S. (1982). Sex roles and societal reactions to mental illnesses: the labeling of "deviant" deviance. *Journal of Health and Social Behavior, 23*, 18–24.

Rossi, A. S. (1964). Equality between the sexes: an immodest proposal. *Daedalus, 93*, 607–652.

Rousseau, A. M. (1981). *Shopping Bag Ladies*. New York: Pilgrim Press.

Sandmaier, M. (1980). *The invisible alcoholics: women and alcohol abuse in America*. New York: McGraw Hill Book Company.

Schuman, L. M. (1978). Patterns of smoking behavior. In M. E. Jarvik, J. W. Cullen, E. R. Gritz, T. N. Vogt, & L. J. West (Eds.), *Research on smoking behavior*, NIDA Monograph No. 17, Washington, D.C.

Selected symptoms of psychological distress. (1970). National Center for Health Statistics Series 11, No. 37. Rockville, MD: HEW.

Seward, G. H. (1946). *Sex and the social order*. New York: McGraw-Hill Book Co.

Shaw, S. (1980). The causes of increasing drinking problems amongst women: a general etiological theory. In *Camberwell Council on Alcoholism: Women and alcohol* (pp. 1–40). London: Tavistock.

Shainess, N. (1984). *Sweet suffering: woman as victim*. Indianapolis: Bobbs-Merrill.

Siegel, R. K. (1977). Cocaine: recreational use and intoxication. National Institute on Drug Abuse Research Monograph Series: *Cocaine*. Rockville, MD: DHEW 119-133.

Simpson, G. M., Varga, E., Lee, J. H., & Zoubok, B. (1978). Tardive dyskinesia and psychotropic drug history. *Psychopharmacology, 58*, 117–124.

Sinclair, A. (1962). *Prohibition, the era of excess*. Boston: Little, Brown.

Smith, D. E. (1984). Diagnostic, treatment and aftercare approaches to cocaine abuse. *Journal of Substance Abuse Treatment, 1*, 5–9.

Szasz, T. (1974). *Ceremonial chemistry. The ritual persecution of drugs, addicts and pushers*. New York: Anchor Press/Doubleday.

The Talmud (The Study of the Mishna) in Hebrew and Aramaic, Babylonian. I. Epstein (Ed.). London: Soncino Press.

Verbrugge, L. (1981). Sex differentials in health and mortality. In A. H. Stromberg (Ed.), *Women, health and medicine*. Palo Alto, CA: Mayfield Publishing Co.

Verbrugge, L. M. (1982). Sex differences in legal drug use. *Journal of Social Issues, 38*, 59–76.

Weitzman, L. J. (1985). *The divorce revolution: the unexpected social and economic consequences for women and children in America*. New York: The Free Press.

Wetzel, R. D. & McClure, J. N. (1972). Suicide and the menstrual cycle: a review. *Comprehensive Psychiatry, 13*, 369–374.

Who works at work? (1977). *ISR Newsletter, 5*, No. 3.

Wilsnack, R. W., Wilsnack, S. C., & Klassen, A. D. (1984). Women's drinking and drinking problems: patterns from a 1981 national survey. *American Journal of Public Health, 74*, 1231–1238.

Winstead, D., Blackwell, B., Anderson, A., & Ellers, M. K. (1974). Diazepam on demand: drug seeking behavior in anxious in-patients. *Archives of General Psychiatry, 30*, 349–351.

Working Woman magazine, March 1985, 33–34.

Zucker, R. A. (1979). Developmental aspects of drinking through the young adult years. In H. T. Blane & M. E. Chafetz (Eds.), *Youth, alcohol and social policy* (pp. 91–146). New York: Plenum.

Zucker, R. A., & Devoe, C. I. (1975). Life history characteristics associated with problem drinking and antisocial behavior in adolescent girls: a comparison with male findings. In R. D. Wirt, G. Winokur, & M. Roff (Eds.), *Life history research in psychopathology* (Vol. 4). Minneapolis: University of Minnesota Press.

Perspectives on Drug Use in the United States

Louise G. Richards, Ph.D.

ABSTRACT. Different views have prevailed within our society that have provided divergent approaches to explain drug use and drug addiction. Many of these approaches have involved medical, sociological and psychological perspectives; moral factors have also been evoked. This paper explores drug use from a different perspective—cultural anthropology. It discusses drug use as a natural result of human technology. Drawing on a theory of culture as communication systems derived from elaborate patterns of behavior, this paper proposes that criminal and medical explanations of drug abuse have inhibited the development of a comprehensive understanding of drug use. It is possible that a "new culture" has developed in which many people anticipate using some type of psychoactive substance, selected from the legal, illicit and prescribed substances, on an "as needed" basis to change mood or feeling-state. These thoughts are elaborated on in the present article.

Drug use and addiction have existed under several different guiding policy assumptions: disregarded as personal eccentricity; labelled as a scourge on the society, especially the criminality and violence attributed to use; believed to be a disease that can be treated and perhaps cured. This paper will explore another conceptualization that may throw additional light on what seems to be an intractable problem. It is a framework derived from cultural anthropology: psychoactive substances as the natural result of human technology, their consumption patterns, and their spread through the population. Drawing on a theory of culture as communication systems derived from elaborate patterns of behavior (Hall, 1959), it is proposed that the criminal and medical conceptualizations have kept us in a defensive posture toward drug use. Consideration of abused drugs and others substances as part of the exploitation system of the society

Louise G. Richards, Potomac, MD 20854.

leads to new insights into the phenomenon. It is possible that a new "implicit culture" has developed in which a large share of the population expects to use some psychoactive substance, selected from among the legal, illicit and prescribed ones, on an "as needed" basis, to change mood or feeling-state. These thoughts are developed further in the sections that follow.

BACKGROUND

The phenomena of illicit drug use and addiction have existed under varied and changing conceptual umbrellas. Assumptions about their nature have differed among professional segments as well as between them and the federal government. Before 1900, there was an outcry against morphine and cocaine, but the public was mainly tolerant or unaware of the amount of these drugs available in nostrums and even physician-dispensed medicine. Starting with the Pure Food and Drug law in 1906, there was greater awareness. The Harrison Narcotic Act of 1914 concluded a decade or more of debate over the wisdom of considering addicts as either criminals or victims of a disease. In the 1920s and until the 1960s, the "hard line" prevailed. Physicians carried out little or no dispensing to addicts, the government's "narcotic farms" were virtual prisons, and mandatory sentences became legal (in 1956). During the Kennedy administration, public attitudes and policy took on a medico-psychological flavor, and in 1970 a new law corrected some inconsistencies in existing law.

The Public Health Service's establishment of community after-care, and more recently, wide availability of treatment programs, were policy manifestations of the belief that drug use and addiction are medical problems, involving, incidentally, psychiatry more than the other medical specialties. Although some treatment modes (drug-free residential treatment, for example) may not employ medical personnel as treaters, there is an underlying assumption that the problem is one requiring "treatment" of the user's personality. Diagnosis, treatment regimens, and follow-up are common terms in much research; government-funded studies are distinctly medical, biological, or psychological in orientation.

The orientation of research is illustrated by the current research topics listed in the 1984 National Strategy (The White House, 1984): biological interactions, brain receptor mechanisms, basic biological and behavior processes; adverse medical consequences, basic abuse and addiction potential of drugs, identification of persons under the influence of drugs, identification of "resistance" factors, and epidemiology. The only types of research even partially socio-cultural in emphasis were cost studies, evaluation of prevention programs, and a residual category of interdisciplinary research. An ironic fact is that many social scientists are conducting research on drug abuse under government sponsorship, but their work goes on under labels of "epidemiology," "etiology," or "prevention."

At the same time that the medical model prevails in research and treatment, enforcement of laws against trafficking continues the effort to reduce the availability of illicit drugs on the street, as well as to intervene in the production of raw materials and illicit manufacturing here and abroad. Enforcement against personal possession does not have a high priority at the federal level, but is carried out at the local level, subject to local politics and policies.

CURRENT OFFICIAL POSTURE

The current official federal posture toward illicit drug use is, expectedly, less yielding than other administrations since 1960. A "drug-free society" is a clearly stated goal, and drug abuse is considered morally wrong. The prevailing attitudes are evident in statements such as:

> Permissive attitudes are giving way to a sense of responsibility. . . . Ending a long period of discouragement and lack of decisiveness, the early 1980s have brought a dramatic change. . . . An important change is the moral confusion previously associated with drug abuse. (The White House, 1984)

The National Strategy contains no definition of "drug abuse" and how it may differ from "use." It is clear that the strategy makes illegal or illicit drugs the objects of the goals of universal personal abstinence and elimination from society. Alcohol is mentioned as a drug "which causes the greatest range of acute and chronic medical and social problems," and the Strategy focuses on it as an illegal drug for youth and as a problem for drivers, and sets a high priority for employee assistance programs. Prescription drugs are mentioned too; the Strategy emphasizes the need to "find ways to reduce the dangers of misuse." However, there is no discussion of the inconsistency in existing laws or enforcement among these types of substances. Tobacco is not mentioned at all.

Although there are more negative tones about drugs in the current administration's statements than in those of several previous ones, the stance is not drastically different. No administration in recent memory has veered from the position that the illicit drugs should be personally avoided and should be removed from sale. Only at the state level (in eleven states) has there been divergence from the position against personal possession of drugs, and only regarding marijuana.

The federal government's posture is an accurate reflection of the views of much of the public, especially those middle-aged or older. They are frightened of illicit drugs but tolerate the more familiar substances, alcohol and tobacco. The view diverges from that of many scientists who see all the substances as drugs with varying effects and adverse consequences. At times it seems as if the two groups are describing entirely different phenomena.

A CULTURAL THEORY

The anthropologist Edward Hall has described a basic cultural activity that encapsulates the popular view of drugs as the enemy: the *defense* system (Hall, 1959). According to Hall, the defense system of a culture involves law enforcement (defense against forces in human society), medicine (defense against disease), and religion (defense against danger in nature and in the individual). Two of these aspects are prominent national strategies in dealing with drug use in this country: law and medicine.

Is the defense system of law and medicine the most realistic category for the drug problem? Has it resulted in creative new directions that have quieted the controversies, lessened the adverse consequences, or lowered the need for costly resources? It seems as if the problem has hardly changed for the better in the last twenty years. As an intellectual exercise, at the least, it might be fruitful to look at another cultural system that could represent the reality in a different way.

In Hall's theory, another system, *Exploitation*, the production and consumption of the material culture, is apt. The production and use of a range of psychoactive substances, including many of both legal and illicit drugs of today, has been going on for millenia. Many of both kinds have been and are grown for commercial profit. The material system view rests on the assumption that consumption occurs as the result of certain universal human needs and desires, regardless of whether the goods produced are in the best interests of all individuals or of the society as a whole. Considering illicit drugs as part of the array of material culture and human technology, including the old, simple forms, as well as modern, complex ones, and considering the effect of this technology on other cultural systems, for good or ill, seems like a reasonable conceptualization to explore.

THE FRAMEWORK OF TECHNOLOGY AND MATERIAL CULTURE

Illicit drugs are used for many of the same purposes and usually in the same ways as the ''domesticated'' consumer products—alcohol and tobacco. Their use has spread in the same ways that use of other consumer products spreads, even though the drugs are available only in the underground market or through misuse of the medical system. When new or previously unknown products such as marijuana come to the attention of the public, they spread very much according to the laws of the diffusion of innovations.

Marijuana had been known in the U.S. for many years, but its use was limited primarily to specific groups of musicians, Hispanic laborers, and ''bohemians.'' In the upsurge of marijuana use in the 1960s, the ''early adopters,'' faculty and graduate students on the East Coast, ''turned on'' other academics, including undergraduate students. High school students emulating college students soon followed. Rural areas and more traditional regions (South and North Central) were next. One researcher called the result ''homogenization'' (Miller et al., 1978). Other drugs have had different diffusion patterns, but all can be traced in similar ways. Even drug combinations such as ''Ts and blues'' mimic the tendency for syntheses of separate elements in the drug industry and in other classes of consumer products.

The taking of illicit drugs mimics, in many ways, the taking of either legal recreational drugs or prescribed drugs. Dosage levels are known or titrated, active ingredients are diluted to suit the individual or the market, different concoctions are labeled like commercial brands, antidotes are known, and much technical information is available by word of mouth.

The spread of a new illicit drug may resemble a disease epidemic in some respects, but it is not the same. Its "hosts" are willing users, not innocent victims of a bacterium, virus, or physical disability. The "vector" (drug) is not an organism to be tracked, but a product that follows the laws of supply and demand, marketing, price and income elasticity, product differentiation, and the other laws of market economics. And unlike disease conditions, use of these products serves functions sought by the users. They have "utility" as other products do, reflected in the reasons users have given in motivation studies. The functions range from recreational to instrumental, the basic one being *a change in mood or feeling state*. That is what is sought in the use of alcohol, tobacco, marijuana, cocaine, and all of the so-called abused drugs (as well as in some other nonsubstance-related activities). The feeling state may at times be secondary to social or symbolic reasons for use, as is true of many consumer products. The fact that use may entail medical hazards does make the act a disease. Andrew Weil (1972) went so far as to propose that the desire to change consciousness is a "basic human appetite" that is satisfied by drugs as well as other activities, and that only one people, the Eskimos, have lacked a traditional intoxicant in their culture.

The basic desire to change one's mood or feeling through the administration of an available substance is a more realistic assessment of the so-called "predisposition" to drug use than are theories of addictive or deviant personality. No theory of drug-prone personality can explain why five percent of college students with marijuana experience grew to sixty percent from 1967 to 1978. The desire exists in many forms, from the hankering of "chocoholics," coffee lovers, and regular cigarette smokers to patients who visit their doctors hoping to relieve pain, depression, or anxiety with a prescription. The desire or "need" for substances may or may not be universal, but there are few individuals or groups that are completely abstinent from all of the wide range of substances that contain weak or potent active agents. The tendency is certainly not new. What is new is the wide range of substances available and the range of feelings that can be brought about with their use.

Beginning with the use of barbiturates and amphetamines, the development of psychotherapeutic drugs has burgeoned into many formulations designed to treat many conditions. Leaving pain medications aside, there are now stimulants, sedatives, hypnotics, tranquilizers, and anti-depressants, all specific for relief or change in mood or feeling state. (Some of these are also specific for certain somatic conditions.) These means for mood change were added to the consumer product array of alcohol, tobacco, tea, and coffee, and usually taken with specific effects in mind: stimulation, relaxation, disinhibition, and euphoria. Generalization is not difficult from one group of these substances to another, and from both to the set of ''mind-substances'' available from illicit sources—marijuana, cocaine, hallucinogens, opium, heroin, and the others that became available since the 1960s. The effects of specific dosages under certain conditions of the legal and prescribed drugs are probably better known by the general public (or available in open literature). Users of illicit drugs must rely on word of mouth or the rarer publications available.

The differences in usage pattern—who uses which drugs—can be mapped in much the same way that market research pinpoints differences in product usage through survey results. *Sources* are a major variable affecting the patterns. An early study by Mellinger (1971) found that types of drugs used by individuals primarily followed lines of source availability. Those who obtained psychotherapeutic drugs from a medical source tended to be older and female; they seldom used drugs from an informal, nonmedical source (friend or relative). Those using drugs from an informal source were younger; they used a wider variety of drugs and drug classes (though less frequently than the prescribed users) and used marijuana more frequently. (Recently young adult professional and business people have become a market for cocaine.) A third model included OTC users who tended to use drugs obtained from neither a medical nor an informal source. If we add to the ''source'' types the users of alcohol and tobacco, we would find the so-called ''straights,'' both younger and older, who use the legal substances but do not go on to the illicit drugs; they are of both genders, but the alcohol users are somewhat more likely to be male. They would be distributed among the first and third model types.

Another later study by Mellinger et al. (1978) demonstrated market segmentation of psychoactive drugs by gender, and also showed the effects of two interesting variables, psychic distress and life crisis. The National Household Survey of Psychotherapeutic Drug Use found that both men and women with high levels of psychic distress and life crises had used psychotherapeutic drugs or alcohol at higher levels than other persons in the year preceding the survey. But alcohol use was much more prevalent among high distress men than it was among high distress women, and women used the prescribed drugs more than men. The authors suggested that "use of medically prescribed drugs and use of alcohol are generally viewed as alternative ways of coping with emotional distress and life crises" (Mellinger et al., 1978, p. 1050).

A MELTING POT OF DRUGS AND USERS

Evidence is mounting which indicates that users are making less of a distinction between licit and illicit drugs in their patterns of use, and that the differences between users of illicit and licit drugs are becoming blurred, especially when prescription drugs are taken into consideration. It appears that large portions of the population consider the entire spectrum of psychoactive substances as available to them, regardless of source, for different effects and different situations. Not only has "homogenization" of users occurred, as Miller et al. (1978) observed, but a potpourri of substances may also have become a possibility for many. Some of the evidence is:

1. Instead of the "heroin addicts," "potheads," "cokeheads," "speed freaks," and other one-drug users, polydrug users are more frequently encountered on the street and in treatment.
2. From the earliest national surveys of drug abuse to the most recent, correlations of illicit drug use with alcohol and tobacco use have been consistently positive for the illicit drug users.
3. Young adults (in their mid-twenties), who had used marijuana in their teens, were more likely to be using legally prescribed psychoactive drugs than those young adults who did not use marijuana in their teens. (Yamaguchi and Kandel, 1984)

The tendency for many Americans to "take" something—coffee, cigarettes, alcohol, marijuana, tranquilizers, cocaine, or even heroin—to change their feeling state fits the conditions for the kind of cultural mode Edward Hall called *implicit* or *informal* (Hall, 1959). Implicit culture is represented by behavior that is widely practiced without self-consciousness, like the syntax of language. The formal culture might come into play occasionally when, for example, coffee was served from a silver service, marijuana passed to a circle of teens at a party, or heroin injected in a shooting gallery. Formality comes into play when someone is caught in possession of an illegal drug. But the implicit culture is there when someone *thinks* of a substance he or she feels is needed to get through a bad time, a good time, or a momentary discomfort. The classic humorous version of this was portrayed by the actors in the film "*Starting Over.*" When the character played by Burt Reynolds collapsed on a mattress in a department store, overcome by anxiety, at least half of the onlookers offered him tranquilizer pills pulled from their purses or trouser pockets. The humor arose from an exaggeration of a recognizable reaction to an everyday situation.

The implicit culture of mood-change-through-substances that we see is an American brand; such a condition would have a different look in a different society. The value placed on freedom in the United States means that enforcement policies leave adult users more or less to their own devices, except when caught in violent or compromising situations. Constitutional freedom of speech means that *High Times* magazine can stay in business, and books on how to smoke marijuana can be purchased. Action against drug-related song lyrics and humor in the mass media has been successful, mainly because of voluntary codes by broadcasters, but scenes of heavy cigarette or alcohol use are very much in evidence.

American-style entrepreneurship is evident in the millions of acres of small plots devoted to growing marijuana illegally, some for profit. And, although age distinctions have faded somewhat, the association of illicit drug use with youth is strong—and youth culture in America is a phenomenally strong influence. The implicit mood-change culture (not to be confused with the drug culture) has a home-grown cast, but like many American products, it is spreading to other countries, and they are struggling with the same dilemmas we have faced for twenty years.

BEHIND MATERIAL CULTURE

Webster's Third Edition defines technology as "the totality of the means employed by a people to provide itself with the objects of material culture." Such "means" involved the application of knowledge to practical purposes'' (another definition in Webster's Third). The essential element of technology is knowledge, but its manifestation is thought of primarily as material—objects, products, substances, machines, systems, whatever has been made or used by humans with their special knowledge, whether newly created or passed down through centuries. The range of technology in use by humans today goes from the most primitive known, making fire, through very old processed materials such as alcohol and tobacco, simple tools such as the axe, still in use, to modern chemical, electronic, and edificial miracles that need no elaboration.

Russell (1972) classified various types of technology, one of which, the ''micro'' type, covers consumer goods. This type of technology, Russell said, usually spreads without planning or policymaking. Regardless of the origin of the goods, the consequences of the spread of these may be ''as far reaching as those of a large scale technical project.'' Usually the influence of a new technology spreads ''gradually, unplanned and undirected'' (Russell, 1972, p. 321). One has only to consider the effects of a minor change in U.S. technology to appreciate that statement: Air conditioning is credited with the migration of millions of people to hotter climates, the continuation of business productivity through the year, and extension of the Congressional schedule into the Washington summer!

Today's illicit drugs are a mixture of technologies—old ones such as the processing of marijuana and opium, and new synthetic methods, such as those used for PCP and LSD. The technology consists not just of the substances and methods of manufacture, but also the methods of use.

The possibilities of mood change through expanded drug technology are startlingly broader and better known than fifty years ago. The means of control of one's own mood is almost as different today as the means of control of interpersonal contact through telephone and international travel through air flight. Lennard's (1971) paraphrasing of Marshal McLuhan's views are relevant:

> Psychoactive drugs represent a new technology. In Marshal McLuhan's terms drugs are a new medium and can be conceived of as an extension of the bio-chemistry of the body in the metaphorical sense that a computer represents an extension of the brain or the nervous system. (p. 70)

McLuhan's concept is all the more interesting in light of the fact that new research on the brain reveals specific receptor sites for drugs that apparently mimic endogenous brain chemicals.

THE DARK SIDE OF TECHNOLOGY

Any citizen of a modern nation who is aware of his or her surroundings knows that when new technology bursts on the scene, it not only changes life, but can create unanticipated negative effects. Since early muckrakers pointed to sweatshops and mine disasters as the price of industrialization, we know that the society continues to be unable or unwilling to control the most "successful" technological innovations. Air pollution and highway accidents are only two but probably the best known unintended consequences of the widespread adoption of the automobile. We cannot imagine living without autos, yet we are making agonizingly slow progress in overcoming pollution and accidents.

The bright picture of expanded psychoactive drug technology has its dark side too. Diversion, clandestine manufacture, overprescribing, overdoses, suicides, and addiction are part of it. A somewhat lighter shade of dark is the quasi-legal use of prescription drugs on the part of patients who extend prescriptions to assure a future supply, lend, borrow, or otherwise use prescription drugs as a household staple.

The dark side of the old technologies of alcohol and tobacco manufacturing are very much in evidence. The negative aspects of both these and legally prescribed drugs are equal to if not greater than those of illicit drugs.

Though we can imagine the society's functioning without tranquilizers, sedatives, hypnotics, antidepressants, and stimulants, no one could seriously recommend banning them. The disruption in physicians' practices, unhappy and ill patients, and disrupted families, to say nothing of bankrupt corporations, would be nearly disastrous. Lennard and associates, in 1971, and many others have written critically about widespread nonrational or excessive prescribing of (primarily) tranquilizers. The situation has improved since 1971. Physicians are more enlightened and in 1973 new regulations limited the length of new prescriptions and the frequency of renewals. Since then Valium has dropped from number one to number four in prescriptions written. No one knows whether this previous wide experience with the effects of Valium will give it a permanent place in former users' drug ''repertoire.''

Several newspaper accounts of unorthodox use of prescription drugs in other countries are reminders of the potential for ''creative'' use of psychoactive drugs. One was a story of German parents drugging their children to improve their examination stamina, and the other was a report of Lebanese citizens surviving the psychological effects of the civil war through the use of (minor) tranquilizers. Though the stories may not be accurate, they are plausible and therefore possible at some time or place.

SHOULD THE DRUG INDUSTRY BE BLAMED FOR DRUG ABUSE?

This was a burning question in the mid-1960s. Many feared that the wide prescribing of psychoactive drugs had been the model for the new drug taking by the young. Youngsters were known to raid their parents' medicine chests for party drugs, or at least newspapers reported so. A few researchers found that children of mothers who took prescribed psychoactives were indeed more apt to be using marijuana and other illicit drugs than were other adolescents. Others (Kandel, 1976, in particular) found that adolescents' initiation into use of marijuana was *not* correlated with mothers' use of prescription psychoactives. (Many studies did show that children of parents who used alcohol or tobacco tended to use illicit drugs more than others.)

Because Kandel's (1976) study was particularly well-designed and carried out, the findings were widely accepted at the time. The results were taken by many as an exoneration of the drug industry. In retrospect, it should not have been surprising that there was no correlation between adolescent marijuana use and parental use of prescription psychoactives. Marijuana was usually introduced by other adolescents, certainly not by parents, and was seldom spread by other family members. Youth adopted marijuana, hash, ''speed,'' and the hallucinogens as ''their'' drugs, symbols of the counterculture and youthful rebellion of the 1960s. Initially, as drugs became popular, youth spurned alcohol and tobacco as the trappings of an older generation, and they also spurned prescription drugs as the trappings of established medicine. So the lack or correlation of adolescent marijuana use and parents' use of prescribed drugs at the time could be attributed to the attempt of youth to differentiate itself from adult society, not by a desire to emulate it. As was noted earlier, however, illicit drug use and prescription drugs were positively correlated in the same individuals as young adults. (Mothers' earlier prescribed drug use was also correlated with young adult women's prescribed drug use [Yamaguchi and Kandel, 1984].)

The researchers who carried out two national surveys of legally prescribed psychoactive drugs found only small proportions of persons who had overused drugs or used them in other than appropriate ways (Mellinger et al., 1978). They pointed out that large proportions of persons with psychic distress had not had drugs prescribed for them. The studies were designed to examine drug use within the context of medical visits, symptoms, and the like, so the obtaining or use of those drugs beyond medical supervision was not likely to be found. The authors considered it serious that many patients underused prescribed drugs, rather than overused them. This attitude of "pharmacological Calvinism," they felt, may have developed in part because of excessive publicity about drug use and addiction.

The precise role of the drug industry and physicians' prescribing in generating the illicit drug problem can never be clearly determined. Many factors have been cited as possible causes, including attitudes toward the Vietnam War, weakening of family life, affluence, and the excess of population entering adolescence. Certainly, the drug industry did provide a backdrop of acceptance of possibilities for mood change that was understood by the general population. It seems likely that the industrial development of new psychoactive drugs contributed in part to the creation of an implicit mood-change culture.

TAKING DRUG HAZARDS INTO ACCOUNT

In considering all psychoactive substances together as a spectrum of material culture, it may appear that the hazards of use of illicit drugs are being glossed over. The rationale used for singling out those particular drugs in modern legislation is their capacity for causing illness, injury, and addiction (plus their lack of use in approved medicine). The real hazards for most of these drugs are evident in the death and emergency room statistics from the Drug Abuse Warning Network (National Institute on Drug Abuse, 1983).

An exception is marijuana, which does not show up as being nearly as lethal or injurious as the others. Along with this picture is the extent of damage known to be done by the legal substances alcohol and tobacco, which is much greater in extent than that of illicit drugs. This inconsistency is part of the dilemma of drug use policy.

As the experience with alcohol prohibition showed, the public's desire for consumption, when combined with other forces, can circumvent and eventually overturn the law despite known hazards of use. Circumvention is taking place with millions of users of illicit drugs today. The nation finally settled for legalization of alcohol with as many restrictions and other control mechanisms as politically feasible to prevent the worst effects. One such restriction was the banning of alcohol to adolescents or young adults below a certain age (set by states and local areas). The restrictions have not been strong enough to overcome the wide extent of damage done by alcohol, but no one knows where to strike the correct balance to make such restrictions work.

Many consumer products survive in the legal market because consumer demand (plus industry pressure) outweighs the concern over hazards. No one can predict whether legalization of any of the currently illicit drugs will occur in the foreseeable future. Changes in drug law seem to come about primarily as the result of political processes. They are affected by intellectual or scientific judgments, but controlled more by professional and business interests.

CONCLUSIONS

The foregoing discussion was undertaken as an intellectual exercise to try to understand illicit drug use with a conceptualization different from the prevailing defensive ones of crime and disease. There are several perceptions resulting from this exercise:

1. The desire to change mood with psychoactive substances is well-entrenched in U.S. society. Different groups meet the desire with different assortments of substances. The group differences seem to be diminishing and substance possibilities expanding.
2. Both old and new technologies have contributed to the psychoactive material culture available today.
3. Technology has a dark side—unintended adverse conse-

quences—and drug technologies are no exception. Although the drug industry cannot be "blamed" for the illicit drug use, it has made the public aware of a wider range of possibilities for mood change.

4. Like many other consumer products, both legal and illicit drugs carry risks if not used carefully. Restrictions, regulations, and other control mechanisms do not completely contain the risks. The political process is dominant in changing the legal status of these substances.

The above descriptions and hypotheses are not intended as arguments for a change in current drug use policy. It is difficult to choose among the arguments that point to inconsistencies in current laws and those against full legalization of currently illicit drugs. The observations are intended primarily as food for thought. It should be mentioned that the results of sociocultural research if not reflected in much of current *policy* are much in evidence in many programs, especially prevention programs.

The revolution in psychoactive drug products is far from over. The possibilities of new drugs that enhance perception, memory, and intelligence, and others that may provide pain relief without addiction potential, are startling in their implications. If they materialize, it is hard to imagine how they can be kept within the bounds of medical practice. More profound insights will be necessary to deal with these exigencies, if they arise.

Robert Frye (1980) has suggested that drug abuse is an example of culture (i.e., drug development) running too far ahead of biological evolution. Drugs today can simulate natural systems like that of the endorphins, thereby "shortcutting" the original biological functions of pain alleviation for man. The implications of this theory too are startling.

REFERENCES

Frye, Robert V. (1980). The sociobiological paradigm: a new approach to drug using behavior. *Journal of Psychoactive Drugs*, 12:21–25.

Hall, Edward T. (1959). *The Silent Language*. Doubleday and Company.

Kandel, Denise B., D. Treiman, R. Faust, and E. Single. (1976). Adolescent involvement in illicit drug use: a multiple classification analysis. *Social Forces*, 55:438–58.

Lennard, Henry L. and Associates. (1971). *Mystification and Drug Misuse*. New York: Harper and Row.

Mellinger, Glenn. (1971). Psychotherapeutic drug use among adults: a model for young drug users? *Journal of Drug Issues*, 274–278.

Mellinger, Glen D., M. Balter, D. Manheimer, I. Cisin, and H. Perry. (1978). Psychic distress, life crisis, and use of psychotherapeutic medications. *Archives of General Psychiatry*, 35:1045–1052.

Miller, J. B., Cisin, I., and Harrell, A. W. (1978). *Highlights from the National Survey on Drug Abuse: 1977*. Rockville, Maryland: NIDA.

National Institute on Drug Abuse. (1984). *Data from the Drug Abuse Warning Network (DAWN) Annual Data 1983*. Statistical Series 1 No. 31 DHHS Publication Number (ADM) 84-1353.

Russell, Bernard H., and P. Pelto. (1972). *Technology and Social Change*. New York: The Macmillan Company.

Weil, Andrew. (1972). *The Natural Mind: A New Way of Looking at Drugs and the Higher Consciousness*. Boston: Houghton Mifflin.

The White House. (1984) *1984 National Strategy for Prevention of Drug Abuse and Drug Trafficking*. Drug Abuse Policy Office, Office of Policy Development, Washington, D.C.: U.S. Government Printing Office.

Yamaguchi, Kazuo, and D. Kandel. (1984). Patterns of drug use from adolescence to young adulthood: III. Predictors of progression. *American Journal of Public Health,* 74:7, 673–681.